PROTECTING CHILDREN

I'm writing this poem for all to see
it's from the heart so hear my plea...
open your eyes go on let's see
stop it happening to them like it happened to me

Poem by Teresa, www.napac.org

Online courses in child protection

This course reader supports the online child protection courses delivered by Akamas in association with London Metropolitan University.

The courses ensure that students are equipped with a working knowledge of child protection procedures and processes. They have been developed to provide consistent and accountable safeguarding training for the wider children's workforce, an estimated population of at least 4 million in England alone.

Currently available courses are:

Protecting Children: Developing basic awareness (Level A)
For anyone whose work, whether paid or voluntary, brings them into contact with children and families, e.g. hospital receptionists, school secretaries, minibus drivers, church workers

Protecting Children: Developing basic skills (Level B)
For anyone working professionally with children and families, e.g. teachers, doctors, social workers, police

For more information, please visit our website at www.akamas.co.uk or call 0845 094 0624.

AKAMAS

LONDON
metropolitan
university

PROTECTING CHILDREN

A resource book and course reader

Liz Davies

AKAMAS

Published by Akamas
www.akamas.co.uk

ISBN-10: 1-905931-01-8
ISBN-13: 978-1-905931-01-9

Printed by Lightning Source

All queries regarding content should be addressed to the author:

Liz Davies, Senior Lecturer
London Metropolitan University
Department of Applied Social Sciences (DASS)
Ladbroke House, 62- 66 Highbury Grove, London N5 2AD
Telephone: 020 7423 0000
Email: e.davies@londonmet.ac.uk

CONTENTS

Contents

Contents

INTRODUCTION: WHAT IS CHILD ABUSE?

Quiz: 40 statements about child abuse

Consider the following statements about child abuse and decide whether they are true or false. The answers are given on page 115. You may choose to complete this quiz again after reading through the book.

	True or False?	True	False
1	It is against the law to hit a child	......	......
2	Most neglect of children is in low income families.	......	......
3	Disabled children have an increased risk of being abused.	......	......
4	Children have to consent to a paediatric assessment.	......	......
5	Children are always video-interviewed about allegations of abuse.	......	......
6	Any child on the Register is monitored until they are 18 years old.	......	......
7	Children exposed to abusive images are victims of sexual abuse.	......	......
8	Repeated sexual abuse of children is uncommon.	......	......

	True or False?	True	False
9	Most child sexual abuse is perpetrated by someone who knows and is close to the child.	......	......
10	Sex offenders are usually mentally ill.	......	......
11	Most women know if their partners are sexually abusing children and do nothing about it.	......	......
12	Children very rarely lie about being abused.	......	......
13	Sex offenders can be cured by therapy.	......	......
14	Female genital mutilation is a crime in the UK.	......	......
15	Children who are abused grow up into abusers.	......	......
16	Child sexual abuse victims rarely get justice through the courts.	......	......
17	It is against the law to hit an animal.	......	......
18	Teenage 'prostitutes' do not fall within child protection procedures.	......	......
19	Children are usually asleep when their parents are fighting.	......	......
20	In one sex abuser's life they may abuse more than 200 children.	......	......
21	Most sex offenders begin offending in adolescence.	......	......
22	Young people often sexually experiment with younger children.	......	......
23	Black children are more likely to be physically abused than white.	......	......
24	Social workers and police often take children into care.	......	......
25	Religious families are less likely to abuse their children	......	......

	True or False?	True	False
26	Sometimes it is better to allow abuse to continue rather than break up a family.	......	......
27	If a child does not mind the abuse they are not harmed by it	......	......
28	Any member of the public can make checks with the Child Protection Register.	......	......
29	'Failure to thrive' in babies may be due to organic causes.	......	......
30	When children go missing they are primarily the concern of the police.	......	......
31	Children in care are over represented in statistics of missing children.	......	......
32	Parents who abuse drugs always neglect their children.	......	......
33	A child of 12 can consent to sexual activity.	......	......
34	Alcohol abuse is a serious cause of violence to children.	......	......
35	If a child tells you about abuse you must ask them to try and explain the abuse to you in detail.	......	......
36	If a child tells you he/she has bruises caused by abuse, you should ask the child's permission for you to look at them.	......	......
37	Social workers must gain the parents consent before interviewing a child about alleged abuse.	......	......
38	The GP's confidential records cannot be shared at a child protection conference.	......	......
39	Children have a right to attend a child protection conference about them.	......	......
40	All forms of abuse include emotional abuse.	......	......

What is child abuse?

Child abuse is a term which describes all the ways in which a child's development and health are damaged by the actions or inaction of others. Usually this means by the actions of adults, but sometimes it may be by the actions of other children.

Often the different categories of abuse overlap and many children suffer the effects of a range of destructive behaviour. In such cases it is important to note clusters of signs as these may assume more significance than one indicator in isolation.

Why refer?

Because:

- children have a right to be safe
- adults have a responsibility to protect children
- abuse is damaging
- child abuse exists in a world of secrecy and silence – the cycle of abuse must be broken
- you only have one piece of the jigsaw – it must be shared
- children rarely lie about having been abused
- an abuser may well abuse many other children who also have a right to protection

What do you need to know?

- What are the different types of child abuse
- The child protection procedures
- How to respond to the child's needs

- How a referral is made
- Your role in child protection
- What to expect of other agencies
- How to gain advice and support for yourself
- How to be sure the child is safeguarded

The four categories of abuse

The following definitions are taken from *Working Together to Safeguard Children.*[1]

Physical abuse

. . . may involve hitting, shaking, throwing, poisoning, burning or scalding, drowning, suffocating or otherwise causing physical harm to a child. Physical harm may also be caused when a parent or carer fabricates the symptoms of, or deliberately induces illness in a child.

Emotional abuse

. . . is the persistent emotional ill treatment of a child such as to cause severe and persistent adverse effects on the child's emotional development. It may involve conveying to children that they are worthless or unloved, inadequate or valued only insofar as they meet the needs of another person. It may feature age or developmentally inappropriate expectations being imposed upon children. These may include interactions that are beyond the child's developmental capability, as well as overprotection and limitation of exploration and learning or preventing the child participating in normal social interaction. It may involve seeing or hearing the ill treatment of another. It may involve serious bullying, causing children frequently

---

1. DfES (2006), also available at www.everychildmatters.gov.
uk/socialcare/safeguarding/workingtogether

to feel frightened or in danger or the exploitation or corruption of children. Some level of emotional abuse is involved in all types of maltreatment of a child, though it may occur alone.

Sexual abuse

. . . involves forcing or enticing a child or young person to take part in sexual activities, including prostitution, whether or not the child is aware of what is happening. The activities may involve physical contact, including penetrative (e.g. rape, buggery or oral sex) or non penetrative acts. They may include non-contact activities, such as involving children in looking at, or in the production of sexual online images, watching sexual activities, or encouraging children to behave in sexually inappropriate ways.

Neglect

. . . is the persistent failure to meet a child's basic physical and/ or psychological needs likely to result in the serious impairment of the child's health or development. Neglect may occur during pregnancy as a result of maternal substance misuse. Once a child is born, neglect may involve a parent or carer failing to :
- provide adequate food, clothing and shelter (including exclusion from home or abandonment)
- protect a child from physical and emotional harm or danger,
- ensure adequate supervision (including the use of inadequate care givers)
- ensure access to appropriate medical care or treatment.

It may also include neglect of, or unresponsiveness to, a child's basic emotional needs.

Significant harm

Significant harm and the likelihood of significant harm are decided by professional judgement. This wide concept of harm is at the core

Significant harm assessment[1]

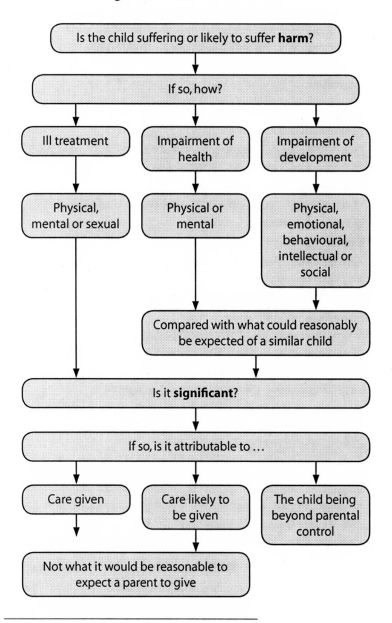

1. From Adcock et al (1991) in Plotnikoff, J and Woolfson, R (1996) *Reporting to the Court Under the Children Act*. London, HMSO

of child protection as outlined in the Children Act. All indicators of significant harm have to be seen in context.

In assessing abuse consideration must always be given to the age and development of the child and to anti-discriminatory practice.

Definitions

Under Section 31 of the Children Act 1989, as amended by the Adoption and Children Act 2002:

* 'harm' means ill treatment for the impairment of health or development , including for example impairment suffered from seeing or hearing the ill treatment of another.
* 'development' means physical, emotional, social or behavioural development.
* 'health' means physical or mental health
* 'ill treatment' includes sexual abuse and forms of ill treatment which are not physical.

Under Section 31 (10) of the Act:
* Where the question of whether harm suffered by a child is significant turns on the child's health and development, their health or development should be compared with that which could reasonably be expected of a similar child.

Useful quotes

"Child abuse consists of anything which individuals, institutions or processes do or fail to do which directly or indirectly harms children or damages their prospects of safe and healthy development into adulthood."

> NSPCC definition, which is broader than the concept of 'significant harm'

"Child abusing behaviour is not an inherent characteristic of individual parents, but an interaction between parents with

unresolved conflicts and vulnerable children, in the context of heightened tension in wider relationships and social stress."

Reder, P, Duncan, S, and Gray, M (1993), *Beyond Blame*

"Multi-agency work starts as soon as there are concerns about a child, not just when there is an enquiry about significant harm... The combination of practice grounded in knowledge and evidence based with the use of finely balanced professional judgement is the foundation for effective social services (professional) practice with children and families."

DoH (2000), *Framework of Assessment for Children in Need and their Families*

"Unless professionals are prepared to face up to the real experiences children suffer we will continue to fail to comprehend the bizarre and horrifying nature of their world and go on ignoring their words. The result will be to increase the danger they face."

Fitzgerald, J (1996), *Listening to Children.*

THE EXTENT OF CHILD ABUSE

"Every full double-decker school bus at the end of the day is likely to be taking home around seven seriously unhappy children. Most of the lower deck would at some time during their childhood have been going home to serious worries. Approximately ten children may be going home to a 'double-shift' of cleaning, laundry, shopping and preparing meals, and two or three will be in fear of violence between their parents while they were out, or of what might happen that evening."[1]

Statistics

In 2000 the NSPCC published a study of 3000 young people aged 18-24 years concerning positive and negative experiences of treatment at home. They found:

- 90% from a loving family background but with large numbers having suffered parental abuse at some point in childhood

- 7% abused physically by a carer

- 6% emotionally and psychologically maltreated

- 6% physically neglected

- 4% sexually abused

- 80% of those physically abused also experienced domestic violence

When one also takes into account the smaller number of cases of children abused outside the family, it is clear that a significant

1. Cawson et al (2000) *Child Maltreatment in the United Kingdom: A study of the prevalence of child abuse and neglect.* London, NSPCC

number of children face repeated pathological and multiple forms of abuse.[1]

Serious abuse is under-reported

In 1995 a collection of various research findings, *Messages from Research*,[2] led to the refocusing of children's services towards children in need and the family support model. Part of the thinking at that time was that too many children entered the child protection 'net' and that social workers were being too interventionist in their approach.

In fact many children who need protection do not access the service they need because the vast majority of serious abuse is unreported or does not get defined into the existing child protection system.

• Very few children report abuse while they are children

• There is a low level of public reporting

• Child victims of domestic violence are often unseen

• Children trafficked for domestic and/or sexual exploitation are kept away from the public eye.

• High level of abuse of children with disabilities and learning disabilities

• High level of abuse of children in institutions – particularly placed out of the locality

• Abuse in middle and upper class families may be undetected and under-reported as professionals focus on socially disadvantaged families

• Racial violence is rarely defined as child abuse

---

1. For more statistical information about child abuse, see www.nspcc.org. uk/Inform/OnlineResources/Statistics/KeyCPStats/Home_asp_ifega26471.html
2. Department of Health (1995)

- Bullying is rarely defined as child abuse
- Thousands of photographs and videos of unidentified child victims are destroyed without child protection investigation
- Children may be abused within families where a parent has a mental illness – often the focus is on the adult rather than the child.[1]
- Abuse of children by women is under reported[2]
- There is a lack of attention to abuse of older children
- Low prosecution levels deter reporting

A focus on prevention is essential to ensure increased reporting of child abuse to enable professionals to protect children. Prevention and protection are not mutually exclusive – both are needed to make sure children are safe.

> Davies, L, 'The difference between child abuse and child protection could be you: Creating a community network of protective adults' *Child Abuse Review*, Vol.13, pp426-432

Abuse of babies

Overall, the 'under-ones' are statistically the cohort/age band most at risk of abuse. They are thus proportionately the largest group on Child Protection Registers. The following statistics are reproduced from the NSPCC's training pack *Fragile: Handle with Care*[3]:

- Of the 2,800 under-ones on Child Protection Registers on 31 March, 58 percent were categorised as neglected, 39 percent

---

1. Falkov, A (1996)

2. Saradjuan, J (1997)

3. NSPCC (2001)

as physically abused, 10 percent as sexually abused and 7 percent as emotionally abused.[1]

- UK children are more likely to be killed in their own home, by members of their own family, than anywhere else in society. This is also true in Australia and the USA. Infanticide is the most common form of child killing.[2]

- The homicide rate for under ones is nearly five times greater than the average, with 59 offences per million of the population of under ones compared to 14 offences per million of the population as a whole.[3]

- 50 percent of victims of homicide by parent or caretaker in a US study were aged 12 months or less.[4]

- 55 percent of murdered infants in the same US study had a history of trauma, for example, broken bones and injuries.[5]

- Although toddlers are just as likely to be injured by aggressive actions from their carers, injuries sustained by infants are more likely to have fatal consequences.[6]

- One survey found that 52 percent of one year old children were hit or smacked weekly or more by their parents.[7] Another found that 75 percent of mothers admitted to smacking their children under the age of one.

1. Department of Health (2000)
2. Brown, K.D, & Lynch, M (1995)
3. Home Office (2000)
4. Brewster et al (1998)
5. Brewster et al (1998)
6. Smithey (1998)
7. Nobes & Smith (1997)

The hidden victims of domestic violence

A study by NCH Action for Children highlighted the serious consequences for children who are exposed to regular and systematic domestic violence. Many suffer a range of emotional and psychological problems. They may become anxious, aggressive or withdrawn, experience disturbed sleep, have problems at school, or find it difficult to form close relationships.

Contrary to common belief, all children are aware of the violence whether or not they have actually witnessed it. The majority overhear the attacks and see the resulting injuries. They see their parents upset and crying and feel the atmosphere of fear and intimidation within the home. It is not uncommon for children also to be victims of the violence.

Research[1] informs us that:

- If a parent suffers physical violence 70% of the children also suffer physical violence

- In 90% cases children are in the same room as the violence or the room next door

- Of children looked after, half have suffered from the effects of domestic violence

- One third of children affected try to protect their mother

- 40% of violence starts with the first pregnancy and escalates during pregnancy. Between 40% and 60% of pregnant women who are assaulted are hit in the abdomen. Pregnant women who are assaulted are twice as likely to miscarry. [2]

- Women suffering abuse are on average beaten 35 times before asking for help and make up to 12 contacts to try and stop it

---

1. Abrahams, C (1994)

2. See www.avenueswomen.co.uk

- As few as 2% of domestic violence cases are reported to police
- Where there is physical child abuse it is also likely that the mother will suffer abuse
- 60% of cases taken to Child Protection Conference include a component of domestic violence

In 1999 a survey of 130 victims of domestic violence found that in 76% of cases where the court had ordered contact with the estranged parent, the children reported they had been abused during contact visits:
- 10% sexually assaulted
- 15% physically assaulted
- 26% abducted or attempted abduction
- 36% neglected
- 62% emotional harm[1]

Women's Aid found that between 1994 and 2004, 29 children from 13 families were killed during contact arrangements. Five of the contacts were court ordered.[2]

Children known or suspected to be victims of domestic violence should always be referred to social services.

The child's viewpoint

The following quotes are taken from *Stop Hitting Mum!* by Audrey Mullender.[3]

- "I've only really ever heard it, but I've never really seen it... I could hear the conversations they were having and mum was saying 'Stop it!' But every time I was crying and... I had to put my hands on my ears because I didn't want to listen."
  – P, age 9

---

1. Radford, L, Sayers, S, and AMICA (1999)
2. Saunders, H (2004) *29 child homicides.* London, Women's Aid
3. Mullender, A (2003)

- "He was just hitting her with his hands and shouting and swearing at her... Just saying all horrible things to her and really hurting her, making her cry and mum couldn't do anything. I just called the police." – S, age 12

- "I used to wet the bed. I think this was to do with their fighting." – S, age 9

- "I've really missed out on my childhood. People say that it is the most carefree part of your life. This was not true for me. This was the worst part of my life – constantly living in fear." – Y, age 16

Disabled children

The inspectors' report *Safeguarding Children*[1] concluded that agencies did not sufficiently prioritise the protection needs of disabled children. However, little research has been undertaken in the UK in respect of disabled children, abuse and protection.

In 2006 the Department for Education and Skills recognised in *Working Together*[2] that disabled children are at greater risk of abuse. The presence of multiple impairments appears to increase the risk of both abuse and neglect.[3] However, significant numbers of local authorities do not collect data about disabled children who are subject to child protection processes.

Children with disability:

- are vulnerable to offenders who think it is safer and therefore more attractive for them to victimise children with a disability

- may have less access to information about abuse and therefore less awareness of how to protect themselves

1. CSCI (2005)

2. DfES (2006), also available at www.everychildmatters.gov.uk/socialcare/safeguarding/workingtogether

3. Further information is available at www.nspcc.org.uk/Inform/OnlineResources/InformationBriefings/Disabled_asp_ifega26019.html

- may be less able to disclose due to disability, for instance through isolation in a residential establishment or through the nature of their disability, e.g. speech impairment

- may be less likely to be believed and may lack the skills and vocabulary to complain

- may be more vulnerable because society's negative attitude towards disability gives the abuser 'permission' to abuse – an attitude of 'What does it matter: the child is inferior anyway.'

- may be more vulnerable because their response to society's negative attitude towards disability is to seek attention and affection

- may be less discriminating about the difference between abusive and non-abusive touching if they are dependant on adults for aspects of personal care

- are sometimes in dependant and powerless situations in relation to adults and may find themselves colluding with the abuse in order to survive

- may have low self esteem and not consider that their own wishes and feelings should be heard

- may be particularly vulnerable to abuse by peers

- may fall through the protective net due to structural divisions in services between those for disabled children and those for child protection

A useful website is www.howitis.org.uk which provides an image vocabulary for children about feelings, rights and safety, personal care and sexuality. This can assist children with communication difficulties in informing adults about any conerns they have about their safety. Other resources are included in the Further Resources section at the back of the book.

Refugee children

In 2005 there were 64,500 children seeking asylum in the UK. The inspectors' report *Safeguarding Children*[1] expressed concern about children in detention centres and stated that children at risk did not receive an adequate response to their needs.

There is much concern about Section 9 of the Asylum and Immigration Act 2004 which is being piloted in the North West, Yorkshire and London. If a family claims asylum and their claim fails then they are denied all benefits. There have been two cases of children being removed from their families in such circumstances through destitution. Such action does not comply with either the UNCRC or the Children Act 1989 and BASW advises social workers not to collude with this practice.

The Early Returns Policy, introduced in 2005, suggested some children being returned to their country of origin. As a pilot this was initially used to send Albanian children back to Albania. It has now been used to return children to Vietnam and the Democratic Republic of Congo. There is serious professional concern about the best interests of these children.[2]

Equally concerning is the number of unaccompanied minors going missing. Operation Paladin-child (2003) examined the cases of all unaccompanied minors at Heathrow airport in a three-month period and discovered 28 who had gone missing and never been found. Following the 'torso' case police asked London schools to check any African boys aged between seven and nine years who were missing from school rolls in a three-month period. A total of 300 were identified as missing and only a few have subsequently been located.[3] These two cases provide an insight into the scale

---

1. CSCI (2005)

2. An article in the *Guardian* covered this story, and is available at politics.guardian.co.uk/homeaffairs/story/0,,1852816,00.html

3. Guidance was issued in 2004 to focus on the needs of children missing from education: *Identifying and maintaining contact with children missing or at risk of going missing from education* (DfES, 2004)

of child trafficking and of the numbers of children who are going missing.

There are no overall statistics about children who go missing and are not found, but the UN estimated the number of trafficked children each year to be about 1.2 million.[1] The UK is a significant destination country for child trafficking.

> - A short video concerning child trafficking is available online at www.endchildexploitation.org.uk/robbiewilliams
> - Mende Nazer has written about her personal experience of modern-day slavery in her book *Slave* (Virago, 2004)
> - For guidance about responding to cases involving trafficked children see The Trafficking Toolkit, available at www.crimereduction.gov.uk/toolkits

Children in prison

The UK has one of the lowest ages of criminal responsibility in the world. From the age of 10 years children can be tried for crimes in adult courts.

The Munby judgement (R. *v* Sec of State All ER 465: 2002) gave local authorities a duty of care to young people in prison but the inspectors' report *Safeguarding Children*[2] said that they "cannot be confident of the response to safeguarding young people in prison". Since 1990 there have been 29 deaths of young people in prison and no public inquiries about these. Between 2000 and 2003, 976 children were held for over one week in segregation (which means at least 23 hours a day in isolation). Children in prison are treated as adults, with adult education teachers and prison officers.

The rate of youth crime has fallen but between 1990 and 2001 the number of 15-year-olds in prison increased 800%. Sentence lengths

---

1. UNICEF UK (2003), *Stop the Traffic!*
2. CSCI (2005)

have also increased substantially and children are imprisoned for non violent crimes in contravention of the UNCRC – breaches of Anti Social Behaviour Orders are a key example. Black children are five times more likely than white children to be in custody.

The Howard League website provides much valuable information on this subject and provides a critique of the rapidly increasing criminalisation of young people by the government.[1] Working Together to Safeguard Children provides guidance on the safety of children in custody in section 11.27.[2]

Child soldiers

The UK signed the Optional Protocol to the UNCRC prohibiting the use of children in armed conflict retaining 16 as the minimum age for recruitment. Yet the UK exempted itself from some aspects of the treaty and allows children under 18 years to be deployed in hostilities in certain circumstances.

The UK has the largest numbers of 16- to 18-year-olds in any European armed force (6,000-7,000 in any given year) and is strongly criticised by Amnesty International and UNICEF. In recent years, the deaths of young people at the Deepcut barracks have received much publicity.

1. www.howardleague.org

2. DfES (2006), also available at www.everychildmatters.gov.uk/socialcare/safeguarding/workingtogether

PHYSICAL ABUSE

Of children who die as a result of abuse about 60% have suffered physical violence and the majority of these cases show a long history of physical assault. Tragedies are often caused through ignorance, for example through shaking injuries or when a child when struck falls and suffers injuries. However, physical injury also includes deliberate acts such as:

- attempted drowning
- poisoning
- smothering /suffocation

Physical indicators

Remember: lists of indicators only flag up possible signs of child abuse. Professional judgement is needed in each case to decide whether a child protection investigation is necessary.

Unexplained bruises, welts, lacerations, abrasions

Location
- Face, lips, gums, mouth, eyes
- Torso, back, buttocks, back of legs
- External genitalia

Shape
- Clustered, forming regular pattern
- Teeth marks, hand prints
- Same as article used to inflict injury, e.g. belt, buckle, flex, stick

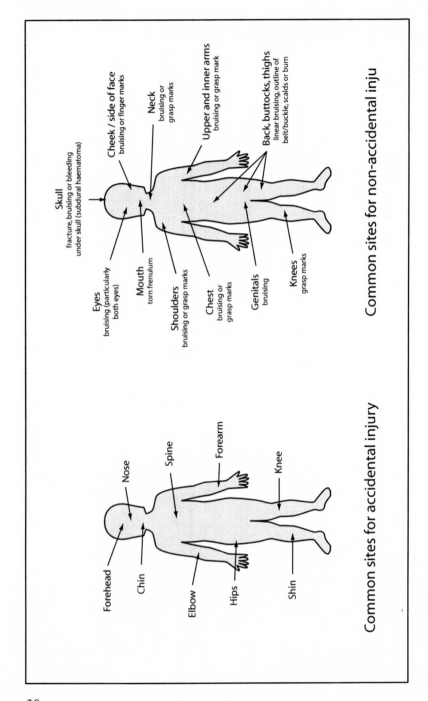

Common sites for non-accidental inju

Skull
fracture, bruising or bleeding
under skull (subdural haematoma)

Cheek / side of face
bruising or finger marks

Neck
bruising or
grasp marks

Upper and inner arms
bruising or grasp mark

Back, buttocks, thighs
linear bruising, outline of
belt/buckle, scalds or burn

Eyes
bruising (particularly
both eyes)

Mouth
torn frenulum

Shoulders
bruising or grasp marks

Chest
bruising or
grasp marks

Genitals
bruising

Knees
grasp marks

Common sites for accidental inju

Nose

Spine

Forearm

Knee

Forehead

Chin

Elbow

Hips

Shin

Unexplained burns

- Small circular burns, particularly on soles of feet, palms of hands, back of buttocks marks
- Immersion burns, clear line of demarcation
- Rope burn on arms, legs neck or torso
- Patterned burns indicating hot object, e.g. electric fire or iron

Unexplained fractures/dislocations

- Skull, facial bones, spine
- Spiral fractures
- Dislocations, particularly shoulder or hips
- Multiple fractures in various stages of healing
- In children under two years, fractures and dislocations *usually* result from blows, throws or other forceful action or from severe shaking

Other forms of injury

- Ingestion
- Bald patches of scalp
- Subdural haematomas (in children under two years)
- Retinal haemorrhages

Health indicators

- Malnutrition
- Eating disorder

Useful questions

It is useful to have the following questions in mind when being alert to the possibility of child abuse:

- What is the injury? Does it appear accidental?

- Where is the injury? Is it in an unusual site?

- When was it caused? Is the age of the injury right?
- How was it caused? What accounts are being given?
- Who caused it? (Both stated and suspected)
- Witnesses? Do the stories tally?
- What action was taken afterwards by the family?

Behavioural indicators

Remember: lists of indicators only flag up possible signs of child abuse. Professional judgement is needed in each case to decide whether a child protection investigation is necessary.

- Wary of adults
- Speaking in monosyllables
- Withstands examination and painful procedures with little response
- Does not turn to parent for support
- Child believes she/he is bad and deserving of punishment
- Constantly trying to please parent
- Role reversal, child tries to care for parent
- Behaviour extremes: aggressive or withdrawn
- Afraid to go home
- Reluctant to undress at school
- Inappropriately dressed to hide marks
- Indiscriminately seeks affection
- Inappropriate or precocious maturity
- Exposure to domestic violence
- Fear of physical contact
- Speaks of being severely punished

Physical chastisement

What is the difference between physical chastisement and physical assault?

In the UK it is against the law to assault an adult or an animal, but Section 58 of the Children Act 2004 allows common assault to be justified as a reasonable punishment for children. This means that children in the UK do not have the same protection under the law as adults from physical harm.

In Scotland it is now illegal to hit a child under the age of three years and in many European countries it is illegal altogether. However, across all cultures, parents and carers discipline their children through the use of physical punishment and not infrequently use implements such as wooden spoons, sticks or flex.

All chastisement may be considered an assault but especially if the punishment causes an actual injury then legal action may be taken. Sometimes children are beaten in ways which leave no marks such as on the soles of their feet or under the hair so evidence of actual injury cannot be the sole criteria to trigger a protective response.

Foster carers are forbidden under the Children Act Guidance to use corporal punishment other than on their own children. Since 1998 physical punishment is forbidden in all schools. Parents cannot delegate their right to physically chastise to nursery staff or teachers. There is clear guidance for staff of children's homes on acceptable forms of restraint.

Statistics

* 90% of parents admit to using physical punishment at some time

* 80% admit to using it within the last year

* 14-15% of parents use implements when hitting their children

* 52% of 1-year-olds are hit at least once a week

- 12% of 1-year-olds are hit daily

- 48% of 4-year-olds are hit at least once a week

- 35% of 7-year-olds are hit at least once a week

- 11% of 11-year-olds are hit at least once a week

- Only 11% of children think smacking is OK and then only for older children[1]

Shaking babies

Shaking babies is very dangerous. It can cause brain damage and can result in long-term disability or death.

The NSPCC training pack *Fragile: Handle with Care*[2] summarises research showing that shaking babies:
- is common, at around 1 in 4000 under-ones
- has a mortality rate perhaps as high as 25 percent
- has a morbidity rate of 50 percent[3]

The most common reason given for shaking a baby is that "it would not stop crying." Showers quotes research revealing that between 25 and 50 percent of interviewees were unaware of the dangers of shaking babies.[4]

Fabricated or induced illness (FII)

Parents and carers may create an illness in their child by making up the signs and symptoms of disease. Such adults may present their child at the local hospital with a breathing or digestive disorder when in fact the adult has invented the symptom to obtain attention

---

1. Collation of research findings by EPOCH

2. NSPCC (2001)

3. Jayawant et al (1998)

4. Showers (1992)

for themselves. In 2002 the government published *Safeguarding children in whom illness is fabricated or induced*, providing detailed guidance on this subject.[1]

Female genital cutting

Young girls age between birth and about twelve years may suffer the mutilation of their genitalia, which is practised by a number of cultures. It is a crime in the UK under the Female Circumcision Act 1985. It is now also illegal for girls to be taken abroad to be victims of this crime. (Female Genital Mutilation Act 2003). However, there has never been a prosecution in the UK.

Linda Weil Curiel represented many children in France.This was the first time children's views about FGC were heard in court and children gained justice.

"Torture is not a culture. I say of course I am entitled to bring you to the courts because if a white child is cut in France it would cause a scandal. Why should we be quiet if it is a black child? She does not suffer less. She is no less entitled to her physical integrity. When she grows up she will not have less need to enjoy the pleasures of life and love. What hurts a white child hurts a black child."[2]

There are different degrees of female mutilation and all cause serious health difficulties particularly in relation to vaginal and urinary infections, difficulty in menstruation, haemorrhaging and post-traumatic stress syndrome. In later life there will be problems with sexual intercourse and pregnancy, though reconstructive surgery may prevent future complications and allow for childbirth by normal delivery.

---

1. Available at www.dh.gov.uk/publicationsandstatistics/
publicationspolicyandguidance/fs/en
2. All Party Parliamentary Group, 2000

There is pioneering work being carried out at some hospitals in conjunction with the African Well Woman Clinics. Women and girls who have already suffered mutilation can seek help from these clinics in absolute confidence.

It is important for professionals to be alert to young girls who may be at risk of being mutilated or who have already suffered. For example, midwives and health visitors can ask mothers if they believe in this practice and then assess the risk to the children. Teachers who notice a child aged 4 or 5 who spends up to 20 minutes passing urine should question whether that child may have been mutilated. If there is any suspicion of female genital mutilation a referral must be made to social services and a specialist advisor from voluntary organisations such as FORWARD should be invited to any strategy meeting.

What about male circumcision?

Male circumcision is not illegal and is not defined as child abuse in the UK. At the same time, it is not recognised by the British Medical Association as a medical procedure.

The campaign group NORM-UK asserts that this is also a children's rights issue when it is:
- a non-medically required procedure
- performed on a child who cannot give consent
- irreversible

They assert that children have a right to body integrity.

Child abuse related to belief in 'possession' or 'witchcraft'

Project Violet is a project initiated by the Metropolitan Police Service to investigate allegations of child abuse associated with faith based rituals. Such abuse usually happens when a carer views a child as different, sometimes because of disability, bedwetting, having nightmares or illness. Believing that this difference is due to the child being possessed or involved in witchcraft, attempts may then made to exorcise the child. Attempted exorcism may involve severe beating, burning, starvation, cutting or stabbing and/or isolation and usually occurs in the household where the child lives. Child protection procedures *must* be applied in these cases.

Two BBC videos on this subject are available online:
- http://news.bbc.co.uk/1/hi/programmes/ newsnight/4667260.stm
- http://news.bbc.co.uk/1/hi/world/africa/4677969.stm

EMOTIONAL ABUSE

There is an element of emotional abuse in all forms of abuse, but some children may be being emotionally abused whilst their physical care may be good.

A child's needs

In order for children to grow and develop healthily the following basic needs must be met.

Need	Detail
Physical care	warmth, shelter, adequate food and rest, hygiene and protection from danger.
Affection	physical contact, holding, stroking, cuddling and kissing, comforting, admiration, delight, patience, time, making allowances for annoying behaviour, general companionship and approval
Security	continuity of care, the expectation of continuing in a stable family unit, a predictable environment, consistent patterns of care and daily routine, simple rules and a harmonious family group
Stimulation of innate potential	by praise, encouraging curiosity and exploratory behaviour, developing skills through responsiveness to questions and to play, promoting educational opportunities
Guidance and control	teaching adequate social behaviour which includes discipline within the child's understanding and which requires patience and a model for the child to copy

Need	Detail
Responsibility	for small things at first, such as self-care, tidying or playthings; gradually elaborating the decision-making the child allowing them to learn through mistakes as well as successes and receiving praise and encouragement to strive and do better
Independence	to make own decisions, first about small things but increasingly about the various aspects of life within the family and society's codes

Elements of active emotional abuse

- Criticism
- Ridicule
- Withdrawal
- Rejection
- Hostility
- Threat
- Exploitation
- Scapegoating

Physical indicators

Remember: lists of indicators only flag up possible signs of child abuse. Professional judgement is needed in each case to decide whether a child protection investigation is necessary.

- Language delay
- Failure to thrive (no organic cause)
- Sleep disorders

- Psychosomatic complaints, e.g. headache, nausea, abdominal pains
- Involuntary twitching of muscles, especially on the face
- Speech disorders

Behavioural indicators

Remember: lists of indicators only flag up possible signs of child abuse. Professional judgement is needed in each case to decide whether a child protection investigation is necessary.

- General developmental delay
- Hyperactive/ disruptive behaviours
- Behaviour extremes, e.g. withdrawn/low self esteem, aggressive/ demanding
- Over-adaptive behaviour e.g. too well mannered
- Inhibited play, poor peer contact
- Unusually fearful of consequences of actions, often leading to lying
- Threatened or attempted suicide
- Scapegoat of the family
- Compulsively clean and neat
- Anorexic/bulimic
- Limited attention span
- Learning difficulties

SEXUAL ABUSE

The key factors in the sexual abuse of children are the abuse of power in the relationship and the child's inability to give informed consent.

The vast majority of sexually abused children are abused by an adult or child who is close to them, i.e. a family member or trusted family friend. Sexual abuse of children may be perpetrated on children of any age – even small babies. Boys as well as girls are vulnerable, and perpetrators include men and women of all ages, classes, cultures and religions as well as some young people who abuse other young people.

Just because a person has experienced sexual abuse does *not* indicate that they will go on to become an abuser. Research has shown that some child sex abusers do have a history of physical or sexual harm, but the vast majority of abused children do not become child sex abusers.

Survivors of sexual abuse tell us that all sexual abuse is damaging, but the trauma may be more severe if:

- the abuse is perpetrated by someone close to the child,
- violence is involved
- the abuse begins at an early age and is repeated over time
- the child is not supported by the non-abusive parent/carer.

Definitions

- A child sex abuser is an adult whose sexual preference is towards children or someone who sexually exploits children.

- "A Schedule One Offender is someone who has been convicted of a crime or crimes against children. However, this term is due to be discontinued and the term 'Risk to Children' is to be used instead."[1]

---

1. DfES (2005) *LASSL*

Types of abuse

Sexual abuse may involve touching and/or non-touching forms of abuse. It includes the following range of abuses which may be accompanied by violence or threats:

- Being taught sexualised language
- Exposure to sexual remarks or suggestions
- Exposure to pornography
- Deliberately exposing an adult's genitalia to a child
- Touching a child's genitals or private parts for sexual pleasure
- Making a child touch someone else's genitals, play sexual 'games' or have sex
- Encouraging a child to watch or hear sexual acts
- Putting objects or body parts (e.g. fingers, tongue, penis) inside the vagina, mouth or anus of the child for sexual pleasure
- Photographing a child in sexual poses
- Inappropriately watching a child undress or use the bathroom
- Rape – oral/anal/vaginal
- Sexual exploitation through prostitution
- Sexual abuse involving animals
- Group sexual activities[1]

How abuse is recognised

The sexual abuse of a child may come to the attention of protective adults in the following ways:

- a direct allegation
- medical presentation
- suspicion through a variety of symptoms

1. www.stopitnow.org

- information gained through police cases involving abusive images of children or sexual exploitation of children
- information gained through knowledge about known or suspected individuals who are a 'Risk to Children' (formerly Schedule One Offenders)

Physical indicators

Remember: lists of indicators only flag up possible signs of child abuse. Professional judgement is needed in each case to decide whether a child protection investigation is necessary.

- Difficulty walking or sitting
- Pain, swelling or itching in genital area
- Bruises, bleeding, lacerations of the external genitalia, vaginal or anal areas
- 'Love bites' or bite marks
- Pain during urination
- Pregnancy
- Vaginal/penile discharge
- Sexually transmitted disease
- Recurrent urinary/vaginal infections
- Constant sore throat of unknown origin
- Genital warts
- Allergic skin reaction to semen
- Torn, blood stained clothing
- Eating disorders
- Bruises, scratches especially to breasts, buttocks, lower abdomen, thighs
- Enuresis or encopresis (bed-wetting or soiling)
- Recurrent abdominal pain/headaches

Behavioural indicators

Remember: lists of indicators only flag up possible signs of child abuse. Professional judgement is needed in each case to decide whether a child protection investigation is necessary.

Reactions similar to those following any other severe stress:

- Regressive behaviour in younger children e.g. bed-wetting
- Fears, nightmares or phobias, e.g. of the dark or particular places
- Running away
- Drug / alcohol abuse
- Mood swings / personality changes
- Depression, anger , aggression
- Deterioration in performance at school
- Suicidal thoughts / attempts
- Self-mutilation

Reactions which may relate directly to sexual abuse:

- Sexualised drawings
- Age-inappropriate sexual play
- Sophisticated or unusual sexual behaviour or knowledge
- Overtly seductive behaviour or aversion to intimacy
- Withdrawal from peers
- 'Prostitution'
- Extreme mistrust
- States he/she is being sexually assaulted
- May feel it is his/her fault
- Confusion about sexual identity
- Cross dressing
- Anger with non-protective carer
- Assumes inappropriate parental role
- Sexually abusive behaviour to other children

- Hints about secrets he/she cannot tell
- Dissociation

The pattern of sexual abuse

The sexual abuse of children often follows a predictable pattern of stages and phases.

1. Engagement or entrapment

The offender initiates the contact with the young person by offering bribes, rewards, special attention or affection. This is referred to as 'grooming' the victim. Sexual abuse is usually well planned by the offender who uses his/her close and trusted relationship to access the child.

2. Sexual interaction

Once the child responds to the special attention, the adult begins some form of sexual activity. The interaction is usually progressive.

3. Secrecy

Once the sexual activity has begun, the adult imposes secrecy by threatening that if they tell:
- no one will believe them
- the young person, family or pets will be hurt
- their family will be broken up
- something bad will happen to the offender
- the young person will be removed from their family
- the young person will be blamed for the abuse.
Many survivors never tell about having been sexually abused

4. Disclosure

Following disclosure the child will be in crisis because of the anxiety caused by the telling of the secret.

5. Suppression

Without adequate family or other support and fearing the threats of the offender the child may retract, withdraw or minimise the disclosure. It is very common for children to retract their disclosure after the initial 'telling.' Children often face disbelief and denial from their family, friends and local community.[1]

Sex abusers' rationalisations about offending behaviour[2]

- I only go so far then I always stop
- I'm drunk
- I'll only do it one more time
- I need to reduce my tension
- She likes it and leads me on
- He won't remember
- She is too young to get pregnant
- She is better than no-one at all
- She is too young to realise what I'm doing
- Nobody will find out, he won't tell
- It's OK, she is my daughter
- It's OK, he's not my son
- She likes me
- He wants my love, affection, attention
- I am lonely – I need love
- He likes being with me – we are close friends
- I am oversexed
- She didn't tell me to stop

1. Summit R (1983) *The Child Abuse Accommodation Syndrome*. Ch.7: 'Child Abuse and Neglect', pp177-93

2. Adapted from Willis, G (1993) *Unspeakable Crimes*. London, The Children's society, p.50

- No one will see me
- I'm teaching him about sex
- It makes me feel better
- He wants me to do this
- I'm in love
- She puts her arms around me and sits on my lap
- I deserve to feel good
- She looks older than she is
- I can't stop myself
- He says 'No', but really means 'Yes'
- I'm not hurting her
- He is very mature for his age
- It happened to me at that age
- She does it for the money
- Some children like sex
- It's more exciting than sex with my partner
- It's OK, she is asleep
- God told me to do it
- He does it with other boys
- In most ways I am a good father
- He's laughing
- If she doesn't want me to, I won't
- My sex life is no-one's business

A survivor's viewpoint

He Took

He may have took something away from me
And that's something I will have to live with
I was innocent and pure and all that it stood for
But he took all that from me
He was the one at blame I didn't ask him to do that to me
Although I often wondered why pick on me
I never asked him to do that to me

He's the one to blame
It's his filth; his squalor; his dirty little secret
His guilt to bear; his shame to wear
At times I may tremor with pain
Both physically and emotionally; feel quite insane
But in time it passes and I carry on
He may have made me a victim
But I made me a survivor
And that he can't take from me

Poem by Netty, www.napac.org.uk

The trauma of sexual abuse

Stigmatisation

. . . occurs when the young person has:
- been blamed by the offender or others
- been forced into secrecy
- not been believed
- been seen as 'damaged goods'
- experienced some good feelings towards the offender

Associated feelings : shame, guilt, being different, low self worth.

Powerlessness

. . . results from the young person's:
- lack of control over their own body
- inability to protect self or stop the abuse
- susceptibility to force or trickery by offender
- inability to make others believe what is happening

Associated feelings: fear, anxiety, shame, inadequacy, need for control

Loss and betrayal

. . . result from the young person's loss of:
- childhood
- self worth
- trust in self and adults
- freedom to develop at own pace
- normal love, affection and nurturing
- intimacy

. . . and betrayal through
- trust and vulnerability manipulated by special adult
- feelings being disregarded
- lack of support and protection from adults
- their own body responding sexually to the abuse

Associated feelings: grief, depression, despair, extreme dependency, mistrust of self (own judgement) and others, anger, hostility, shame, guilt

Sexualisation

. . . occurs through:
- rewarding of inappropriate sexual behaviours
- meeting non-sexual needs through sexual behaviour
- sexual activity being conditioned with negative emotions and memories

Associated feelings: confusion about sexual identity and norms, confusion of sex and love and non-sexual needs, confusion about body and arousal sensations, aversion to sex and intimacy, normal curiosity is stifled[1]

---

1. Finkelhor, D (1986) *A Sourcebook on Child Sexual Abuse*. Newbury Park, Sage

The impact on emotional development

Sexual abuse impacts upon a young person's emotional growth and development in additional ways, and those abused may display any or all of the following characteristics:

1. **Role reversal** – This occurs when the young person is expected to care for or meet the needs of adults

2. **Silence and deception** – This arises out of the strain of carrying the burden of the secret

3. **Regression** – Sexual abuse may arrest the young person's emotional development at the stage the young person was in at the time of the abuse. Therefore behaviours may be exhibited which are younger than their chronological years.

4. **Sexuality** – Fear of sexual contact with people of the same gender as the abuser

5. **Memory loss** – Memories of the abuse or associated people, events or places may remain buried until the person is strong enough to recall them.

6. **Attachment disorder** – This is the young person's fear of closeness and further abuse

7. **Dissociation / Multiple Personality Disorders** – This occurs when abuse is so severe that the child separates themselves psychologically from the experience. Children may then form a new personality to protect themselves from pain.

Child abuse and information communication technology (ICT)

The internet is now widely used by child sex abusers. Adults who are protectors of children need to be aware of this misuse of all types of information technology, so that they can act to protect children and young people from sexual exploitation and abuse.

Why do child sex abusers make use of the internet?

There are a number of reasons why the internet is misused by abusers:

* The internet is widely available to both abusers and children and young people so they can make contact with many children and young people, and search out those who are vulnerable.

* It is easy to be anonymous
    - The abuser can pretend to be someone else, perhaps someone younger, or someone they know will be specially attractive to a particular child
    - They can try to avoid detection by setting up bogus email accounts
    - They can make multiple different contacts by setting up bogus personas in chat rooms

* They can abuse children without leaving the safety of their own homes

* They can feel part of a network or community of similar people

* They can use the internet to recruit new abusers to the network, including people who have not previously abused children

What do child sex abusers do when they misuse the internet?

Abusers are always thinking of new ways to misuse the internet. These include using chat rooms, instant messenger, blogs, forums or bogus email accounts to:

- share information with other abusers
  - Exchanging indecent photographs or pseudo-photographs (constructed images made to look like photographs)
  - Sharing tips on how to avoid being caught
  - Sharing ideas on how to groom children more effectively
  - Exchanging information about children

- contact children and young people to groom them for abusive relationships

- carry on an abusive relationship with a child or children

What is online grooming?

"A course of conduct enacted by a suspected child sex abuser, which would give a reasonable person cause for concern that any meeting with a child arising from the conduct would be for unlawful purposes"[1]

Abusers may do some or all of the following:

- Search for children or young people who are looking for a friend

- Build trust with the child, pretending to be the sort of person the child would like to have as a friend

- Gradually build intimacy and then expose the child to obscene material

- Ask the child to make and transmit pornographic images of themselves or themselves and others

---

1. Home Office (2002), *Protecting the Public*

- Ask the child to perform sexual acts live in front of a webcam

- Use blackmail and guilt to force the child to meet them

These activities cause significant harm to children and young people. Misusing the internet in this way is child abuse.

- To report online abuse of children contact the Internet Watch Foundation – www.iwf.org.uk, Tel: 01223 237 700.
- www.thinkuknow.co.uk has a wide range of information on this subject, including advice for young people

---

Children who sexually abuse other young people

In cases of sexual abuse of children by children, the alleged perpetrator must also be considered as a possible victim of abuse themselves. The protection needs of all the child victims of the alleged perpetrator must be assessed. *Working Together to Safeguard Children*[1] provides guidance on responding to peer abuse in section 11.32.

In this difficult area of work, it is important to recognise the difference between normal sexual experimentation between children and sexual abuse of one child by another. The Bichard Inquiry[2] recommended the implementation of the Sheffield protocol as a means of assessing young people who sexually abuse. This assessment structure is not definitive but is a guide to multi-agency professional analysis.

---

1. DfES (2006), also available at www.everychildmatters.gov.uk/socialcare/safeguarding/workingtogether

2. www.bichardinquiry.org.uk

The Sheffield protocol

1. Age differential: There would be great concern if the age difference was more than two years. If the abuser is post-puberty and the victim pre-puberty there is also cause for concern. The greater the age difference the more likely it is that abuse has occurred.

2. Power differentials: Non-consensual sex is always abusive but the power relationship between the abuser and the victim is important and may outweigh the age differential.

3. Sophistication of activity: Is the type of sexual activity age-appropriate or does it show 'excessive' knowledge? Is it in any way ritualistic or unusual?

4. Consent or complaint: Did both parties consent? Or was one party compliant or co-operating because of age or power differentials? How did the activity come about – in what circumstances?

5. Persistence of activity: How often and for how long does/did this happen? Persistence may suggest abuse but does not always.

6. Changes of activity: Does the pattern of activity change over time, e.g. become more frequent? Are there regular patterns with several partners?

7. Overt aggression: This would usually indicate an abusive relationship.

8. Experience of receiving person: Is it seen as abusive by the recipient – or is the recipient blaming her/himself for what has happened? Both situations are likely to indicate abuse.

9. Attempts to secure secrecy: If there have been attempts to secure secrecy, the reasons for this need clarifying. Secrecy does suggest abuse, although young people may be secretive abut mutual and consenting behaviour for other reasons.

10. How was the activity revealed: Was there a disclosure following upset or difficult behaviour? Or was it an inadvertent comment which led to disclosure? Was it the 'abuser' or the 'victim' who disclosed?

11. Any 'target' victims: Are there common characteristics of age, sex or vulnerability in victims? Common features may indicate a target group which is likely to means abuse.

12. Nature of fantasies: Those with a number of abusive-style fantasies are perhaps more likely to express these in abusive situations. Fantasies give a clue to self-image, views about sex and the nature of sexual interest.

Children abused through prostitution

Safeguarding children involved in prostitution[1] provides guidance about how agencies should work together to:

- recognise the problem

- treat the child primarily as a victim of abuse

- safeguard the child involved and promote their welfare

- prevent further abuse

- provide children with opportunities and strategies to exit from prostitution

- investigate and prosecute those who coerce, exploit and abuse children.

Only when police and social workers work together can young people be protected from child sex abusers. The information gathered from the young people must be collated with that known to police about the alleged abusers.

---

1. Department of Health (2002)

Barnardo's produce excellent materials to assist in understanding this aspect of child abuse:

- *Whose Daughter Next?* – a video and booklet describing how a child sex abuser targets a young girl and exploits her through prostitution

- *No Son of Mine* – a video and booklet addressing the abuse of boys by child sex abusers

Both explain the slow grooming process by which abusers lure the young person into the abusive network.

Forced marriage

A forced marriage is a marriage conducted without the full consent of both parties and where duress is a factor. In 2004 the definition of domestic violence was extended to include acts perpetrated by extended family members as well as intimate partners. Forced marriage and other so-called 'honour' crimes, which can include abduction and homicide, now come under the definition of domestic violence. Many of these acts are committed against children. Advice should always be sought by professionals dealing with such cases as the risk of harm to the child is high.

The government's Forced Marriage Unit has produced guidelines on how to identify and support young people threatened by forced marriage, which are available at www.homeoffice.gov.uk/comrace/race/forcedmarriage/index.html. Advice may be sought from the Forced Marriage Unit on 0207 008 0230.

NEGLECT

Neglect results from the failure to meet the basic needs of a child: the need for food, warmth, clothing, shelter, consistent care-taking and protection from danger. There are often a number of these unmet needs in one case, making communication between agencies extremely important if serious cases of neglect are to be investigated speedily and effectively.

If a child is failing to thrive it is important to first establish whether or not there is a physical cause. Paediatricians will usually be able to establish whether or not the failure is likely to be due to significant harm.

Some neglect may be defined as criminal, which is why it is always important to reach agreement with the Police Child Abuse Investigation Team about whether a case reaches the threshold for criminal proceedings.

The neglect of children takes place in all socio-economic classes and is not, as is commonly assumed, confined to children in the low socio-economic groups.

Physical indicators

Remember: lists of indicators only flag up possible signs of child abuse. Professional judgement is needed in each case to decide whether a child protection investigation is necessary.

- Underweight, poor growth pattern
- Constant hunger
- Poor physical hygiene: severe nappy rash, skin rashes, dirty, thin hair, cradle cap, thickened nails, untreated injuries
- Fatigue, listlessness, lethargy
- Recurrent and persistent minor infections
- Frequent attendance at Accident & Emergency department

- Failure to thrive with no organic cause
- Alcohol / drug / substance abuse

Behavioural indicators

Remember: lists of indicators only flag up possible signs of child abuse. Professional judgement is needed in each case to decide whether a child protection investigation is necessary.

- Dull, inactive
- Rocking, head banging
- Pale and listless, unkempt
- Begging or stealing food
- Lack of access to required medical care
- Frequent absence from school, truanting
- Leaving school late
- Inappropriate clothing for the weather
- Squinting at the board, dental problems
- Says there is no-one to care for him/her
- Caring for siblings, carrying parental responsibilities
- Socially challenging behaviour
- Self-mutilation
- Lack of supervision

What about 'home alone?

There is no legal age at which a child should not be left alone. However, on the basis of professional judgement, it can be defined as neglect depending on the circumstances. Parents can be prosecuted under the 1933 Children and Young Persons' Act if they leave their child inadequately supervised and it is considered that they are guilty of "wilful neglect in a manner likely to cause unnecessary suffering or injury to health". This law is used particularly when a child is harmed as a result of being left alone. However, it is always important to have a strategy discussion in these cases to explore and evaluate the risks to the child.

Percentile charts

These charts are used by doctors, nurses and health visitors to record a child's height weight and head circumference and to make comparisons over time. Curved lines on the chart show the average measurements for a particular age as well as the upper and lower normal limits.

Sample percentile growth chart

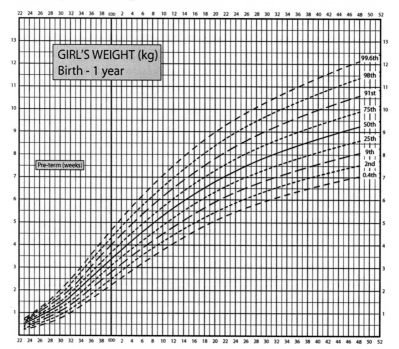

ORGANISED ABUSE

"Abuse involving one or more abuser and a number of related or non-related abused children and young people. The abusers concerned may be acting in concert to abuse children, sometimes acting in isolation, or may be using an institutional framework or position of authority to recruit children for abuse"

DoH (2006), Working Together to Safeguard Children[1]

When any agency reports a situation of organised abuse, named officers in the police and social services will be appointed to co-ordinate the case. A special strategy meeting will be urgently convened involving senior managers.

Organised abuse may involve numbers of child victims and numbers of perpetrators. These investigations are complex and often cross local authority boundaries. Sometimes abuse networks extend outside the country.[2]

It is extremely difficult for children to talk about being a victim of organised abuse. Keeping the child safe during organised abuse investigations is particularly important.

Early indicators

Remember: lists of indicators only flag up possible signs of child abuse. Professional judgement is needed in each case to decide whether a child protection investigation is necessary.

- Child gives clues, whether verbal or non-verbal, about sexual activities

---

1. DfES (2006), also available at www.everychildmatters.gov.uk/socialcare/safeguarding/workingtogether
2. Home Office/DoH, (2002)

- Inexplicable breakdown of the child's world, for example:
  - suspension from school following emotional or aggressive outbursts
  - atypical parental 'over-reactive' behaviour
  - child withdraws from peer group
- Child is exposed to inappropriate sexual material
- Child is introduced to adult activities – alcohol, drugs, crime, abusive images
- Child goes 'missing' or runs away & there is little understanding of the whereabouts
- Child shows unpredictable and inexplicable fears
- Involvement of known 'risk to children' individuals (formerly called schedule one offenders) in the child's life
- Child has access to 'rewards' – money, clothes etc.
- Child seeks out sex phonelines, abusive images, etc.
- Child has intimate knowledge of adults' lives which extends beyond the expected boundaries of the relationship

---

Medical indicators

Remember: lists of indicators only flag up possible signs of child abuse. Professional judgement is needed in each case to decide whether a child protection investigation is necessary.

- Evidence of forced injection, ingestion or other application of drugs, especially muscle relaxants, hallucinogens or anaesthetics
- Evidence of the forced ingestion or external application of non-food substances, e.g. human or animal faeces/urine
- Evidence of the use of implements in the abuse
- Indication of violence, e.g. strap marks to wrists or ankles, marks around the throat

- Evidence of more than one perpetrator having been involved in the abuse (through evidence of sexual abuse or physical assault and also through forensic retrieval)
- Child is extremely afraid of the examination or the photographer
- Evidence of mutilation
- Evidence of sexual activities with animals, e.g. animal hair, blood, semen

---

Other indicators

Remember: lists of indicators only flag up possible signs of child abuse. Professional judgement is needed in each case to decide whether a child protection investigation is necessary.

- Disclosures from the child/children
- Allegations received from the family, community, professionals, etc.
- Police intelligence about abusive images of children or known 'risk to children' individuals (formerly called schedule one offenders)
- Evidence obtained through police surveillance or searches, e.g. photographs/videos
- Child sexually abused in group context
- Young people abusing other young people in a group context or in the presence of adult
- Young person encouraging other young people to become involved
- Use of photography, video or computer pornography in the abuse
- Abuse takes place in a number of different locations
- Adults attempt to change child's name or obtain possession of the child's passport

- Child has heightened level of fear and of the usual indicators of sexual abuse, e.g. attempted suicide, self harm, dissociation, eating disorders,
- Danger-seeking behaviour:
- Alcohol, drug or solvent abuse
  - Involvement in criminal activities
  - Arson
- Known connections between child sex abusers and family members
- The child, family or professionals become victims of threats
- A suspected adult breaks normal boundaries of relationship in order to access the young person
- Adult takes child to isolated places, e.g. caravans, boats
- Child repeats adult terminology and statements indicative of adult power over child
- Child has confused sexual identity, e.g. may say he/she is 'not gay' and yet be involved in homosexual relationships
- Sexual activities involving animals
- Sexual activities involving the use of rituals, costumes, chanting
- Evidence of cult involvement

Operation Orchid

Operation Orchid was one joint investigation of Organised Abuse by police and social workers. A number of sex offenders had abducted, sexually abused and murdered a number of children in the London and Essex areas. The following poem was written by a detective who worked on this case.

> *Who will cry for Orchid's children*
> *the ones beneath the ground,*
> *Who will cry for the missing ones*
> *over bodies never found?*

Who will pray for Orchid's children
the young lives all cut short,
Who will pray that the guilty
will, eventually, all be caught?

Who will remember Orchid's children
as the memories grow dim,
Who will remember the nameless ones
and keep them alive within?

Who will think of Orchid's children
when this work is done,
Who will think about each one of them
in the years that are to come?

Who will cry for Orchid's children
long into the night,
Who will cry for Orchid's children
with tears kept out of sight?

I will.

from *Lambs to the Slaughter*[1]

---

1. Oliver, T, and Smith, R (1993)

LEGISLATION, POLICY AND STATUTORY BODIES

United Nations Convention On The Rights Of The Child 1999

In the current climate, where the UK is not complying with some aspects of the UNCRC, it is important to have knowledge of the relevant articles of the Convention.

No.	States that...
1	The UNCRC is for children and young people aged 18 years old and under.
2	The UNCRC is for all children and young people.
3	All organisations concerned with children and young people should work towards what is best for each child.
5	Government should respect the rights and responsibilities of families.
7,8	Children have the right to a name, identity and family.
9	Children have the right to remain with their family unless it is in their best interests to be separated from them.
10	If the family live in different countries the child and his/her family has the right to travel between them so that they can stay in contact.
11	The government must help stop children and young people being taken out of the country.

No.	States that...
12	Children have the right to have a say about decisions that affect them and have their opinion heard.
16	Children have the right to privacy.
18	Both parents share responsibility for bringing up children and young people and the government should help parents.
19	Government should make sure that children and young people are protected from abuse, neglect and being harmed by the people looking after them.
20	If the child cannot be looked after by parents, she/he has the right to be looked after by people who respect his/her language, culture and religion.
22	Refugee children and young people should have the same rights as children and young people born in the country.
23	Children and young people who have a disability should have care and support so they can lead full and independent lives.
32	The government should protect children and young people from work that is dangerous or might harm their health or education.
33	The government should protect children and young people from dangerous drugs.
34	The government should protect children and young people from sexual abuse.
35	The government should make sure that children and young people are not sold or taken out of the country.
36	Children should be protected from any activity that could harm their development.
37	Children who break the law should not be treated cruelly. They should not be put in prison with adults and should be able to keep in contact with their families.

No.	States that...
38	Governments should not allow children and young people under 16 years old to join the army. Children and young people in war zones should get protection.
39	Children who have been neglected or abused should get special help to get back their confidence and self-respect.
40	Children accused of breaking the law should get legal help. Prison should only be used for the most serious crimes.

The Children Act 1989 (England and Wales)

All child protection work is conducted within the context of the Children Act 1989.

Principles of the Act

- The best interests of the child are paramount
- All interventions under the Act should consider:
  - the wishes and feelings of the child in the light of their age and understanding
  - the racial, cultural, linguistic and religious background of the child
  - the child's educational, emotional and physical needs
  - whether there is significant harm or the likelihood of significant harm
- Agencies should, where possible, work in partnership with the child's parents
- Children should preferably remain within the care of their family
- Help should be provided to families where children are in need

Relevant sections

Section 17

Gives local authorities the duty to safeguard and promote the welfare of children in need through the provision of services if without such services:

- children are unlikely to achieve or maintain a reasonable standard of health and development
- health and development is likely to be significantly impaired

Section 20

Allows for a voluntary agreement between parents and local authorities for the child to be accommodated. This section emphasises the partnership principle of this Act and the numbers of children in care on this basis has increased.

Section 25

Allows a child to be placed in secure accommodation if that child:

- has a history of absconding and is likely to abscond from any other description of accommodation
- is likely to suffer significant harm if he/she absconds
- is likely to injure him/herself or others if kept in any other accommodation

This section is used only in exceptional circumstances and the human rights of the child must be balanced with their need for safety.

Section 31

Provides for the court to make a Care or Supervision Order if it is satisfied that the child is suffering or likely to suffer significant harm. A Supervision Order places a child under the supervision of a local authority supervisor to "advise, assist and befriend" the child. This provides an opportunity to monitor the welfare of the child.

Section 44

Allows an Emergency Protection Order to be obtained by social services in order to make a child safe. This lasts up to 8 days and may be extended for no more than an additional 7 days. There must be reasonable cause to believe the child is likely to suffer significant harm if:

- the child is not removed
- the child does not remain in the place in which he/she is being accommodated.

Conditions may attach to an EPO such as a paediatric or psychiatric examination or a formal child interview.

Section 46

Allows the police to use their powers of protection to remove a child from home for up to 72 hours in an emergency.

Section 47

Requires that, if a local authority has reasonable cause to suspect that a child who is living or found in their area is suffering or is likely to suffer significant harm, they must make such enquiries as they consider necessary to enable them to decide whether to take any action to safeguard or promote a child's welfare.

Section 50

Provides for a Recovery Order which enables local authorities to remove a child who is on a Care Order. They must have reason to believe the child:

- has been unlawfully taken away or is being unlawfully kept away from the person responsible for their care
- has run away or is missing

The Children Act 2004 (England and Wales)

In 2003 the Green Paper *Every Child Matters* introduced a new way of thinking about the protection of children, with an emphasis on prevention.[1] Proposals were introduced to create Children's Trusts and restructure the provision of children's services. The central government responsibility for protecting children transferred to the Department for Education and Skills and the post of Minister for Children was created. Services are now to be delivered by multi-agency teams working within Children's Centres for the younger children and Extended Schools for those over five years old.

The Children Act 2004 places a duty on services to ensure that every child, whatever their background or circumstances, has the support they need in order to:

- be healthy
- stay safe
- enjoy and achieve through learning
- make a positive contribution to society
- achieve economic well-being.

It also requires each Local Authority to establish a Local Safeguarding Children Board (LSCB).

The Children's Commissioner

In March 2005 the Government appointed England's first Children's Commissioner. The role aims to give a national voice to all children and young people, especially the disadvantaged and the vulnerable.

Independent of government, the Commissioner's remit is to promote awareness of views and interests of children. He raises the profile of the issues that affect and concern children in England, and promotes awareness and understanding of their views and interests

1. Full details of the *Every Child Matters* agenda are available at
www.everychildmatters.gov.uk

among all sectors of society, both public and private. This involves working closely with organisations whose decisions affect all aspects of children's lives, including the police, schools, hospitals and voluntary groups.

As part of his broad remit and function, the Commissioner works within the framework of the five Every Child Matters outcomes. These outcomes complement the rights under the United Nations Convention on the Rights of the Child, to which the Commissioner must have regard.

In his first report he stated concern about

- the negative portrayal of children in the media,
- the inappropriate use of Anti-Social Behaviour Orders against children and young people especially those with learning disabilities
- bullying
- children's rights to confidentiality within information sharing systems
- the wellbeing of asylum seeking children kept in detention centres[1]

Common Assessment Framework

As part of *Every Child Matters*, all local authority areas are expected to implement the Common Assessment Framework (CAF), between April 2006 and the end of 2008. It is intended to provide a simple, non-bureaucratic process for a holistic assessment of a child's needs, taking account of the individual, family and community and is proposed to be particularly suitable for use in universal services, i.e. health and education.[2]

Integrated Children's System

The DoH and the Welsh Assembly Government have developed a system for social services managers and practitioners to improve the

---

1. See www.childrenscommissioner.org for more information

2. For more information see: www.everychildmatters.gov.uk/deliveringservices/caf/

outcomes of their work with children and families. It builds upon previous developments such as the Assessment Framework and the Looked After Children materials and offers a single approach to undertaking the key processes of assessment, planning, intervention and review.[1]

It is planned to replace the Child Protection Register with ICS. This would be highly controversial given the research findings which have proven the central role of the Child Protection Register in safeguarding vulnerable children. (Reder, P, Duncan S and Gray M: 1995) The majority of children who die as a result of child abuse have not had their names placed on the Register and have not been defined as in need of child protection planning. Victoria Climbié was one such child. Her case was defined as 'family support' rather than 'child protection.'

- Munro, E (2003) 'This would not have saved Victoria'. *Society Guardian*, 10 September

- Reder, P and Duncan, S (2004) 'Making the Most of the Victoria Climbié Inquiry Report' in *Child Abuse Review*, Vol.13, pp95-114

- Parton, N, Paper to second phase of Victoria Climbié Inquiry, Seminar 1 (available on the Inquiry website at www.victoria-climbie-inquiry.org.uk)

The Children's Database

Proposals to introduce a database for every child in the UK and to record child 'concerns' has raised issues of children's rights and civil liberties. The focus on 'concern' has shifted the focus of intervention away from the Children Act 1989 definition of 'actual or likely significant harm'.

The concept of concern has not been legally defined but suggests a low threshold and it is feared that professionals will be over-

1. For more information see www.dfes.gov.uk/integratedchildrenssystem/about/

whelmed with low level referrals and less able to prioritise and focus on the most high risk child protection cases. The effectiveness of technology in protecting children is also questioned.

For an analysis and critique of government plans to introduce a database for every child, see the ARCH website at www. arch-ed.org

Working Together to Safeguard Children 2006

This national guidance outlines arrangements for co-operation between agencies concerned with the welfare of children for their protection from abuse. The guidance recognises that:

* it is only when agencies work together that children have a chance of being protected.

* no one agency carries total responsibility for child abuse. Each agency has prime responsibility.

* no one should assume that another agency must be dealing with the problem as this may lead to a gap in service and may well place children at risk.

* *Working Together* effectively requires commitment, an open attitude and a willingness to learn from each other

Everyone working with children and families should have access to their local procedures. These will clarify the role of each person involved in working together to keep children safe from harm.

Local Safeguarding Children Boards (LSCBs)

Membership

Statutory members of the LSCB are:
- district councils in local government areas which have them
- the Chief Officer of Police for any police area falling within the authority
- the local Probation Board Youth Offending Team
- Strategic Health Authorities and Primary Care Trusts
- NHS Trusts and NHS Foundation Trusts
- Connexions Service
- CAFCASS (Children and Family Courts Advisory and Support Service)
- the governor or director of any Secure Training Centre in the area of the authority
- the governor or director of any prison in the authority area which ordinarily detains children.

The local authority should secure the involvement of other relevant local agencies and organisations. These should include:
- local schools and FE Colleges
- Sure Start children's centres
- voluntary and community sector organisations
- the NSPCC and bodies providing specialist care to children with severe disabilities and complex health needs
- the armed forces and immigration and asylum support agencies (in areas where they have significant local activity)

Core objectives

The core objectives of the LSCB are set out in section 14(1) of the Children Act 2004 as follows:

- to co-ordinate what is done by each person or body represented on the Board for the purposes of safeguarding and promoting the welfare of children in the area of the authority;
- to ensure the effectiveness of what is done by each such person or body for that purpose.

Functions

- Developing policies and procedures for safeguarding and promoting the welfare of children, including on:
  - action where there are concerns, including thresholds
  - training of persons who work with children
  - recruitment and supervision
  - investigation of allegations
  - privately fostered children
  - co-operation with neighbouring authorities
- Participating in the planning of services for children in the area of the local authority
- Communicating the need to safeguard and promote the welfare of children
- Procedures to ensure a co-ordinated response to unexpected child deaths
- Monitoring effectiveness of what is done to safeguard and promote the welfare of children
- Undertaking Serious Case Reviews
- Collecting and analysing information about child deaths

The Child Protection Register

What is it?

It is a register of children (for the purposes of registration, children include those under the age of 18 years and unmarried) for whom there are currently unresolved child protection issues and for whom there is an inter-agency child protection plan.

The Register facilitates communication between professionals likely to be involved in cases of suspected child abuse and the protection of children. It also provides a method of measuring the size of the protection task

The decision about placing a child's name on the Register is made at a Child Protection Conference. This conference provides the prime forum for professionals and the family to share information and concerns, analyse and weigh up the level of risks to the children and make recommendations for action.

Any enquiries of the Register must be agreed by the Custodian and access is on a strictly 'need to know' basis.

Who is on the Register?

In 2005 there were 25,900 children on Child Protection Registers in England (a 26% decrease since 1995.) The categories for physical and sexual abuse have almost halved since 2001. Registrations in the category of neglect have also reduced but the category of emotional abuse has increased.[1]

Government targets aim to reduce these numbers, assuming that re-registration assumes a mistake was made the first time round in removing the child's name from the Register. However, another school of thought would suggest that re-registration may indicate good practice in re-evaluating cases and examining new information.

The numbers on the Register do not reflect the numbers of children being abused in the UK.

1. www.nspcc.org.uk/Inform/OnlineResources/Statistics/ChildProtectionRegister Statistics/England_asp_ifega26430.html

Multi-Agency Public Protection Arrangements (MAPPAs)

Also known as Jigsaws, MAPPAs were established following the Sex Offenders Act 1997 (they do not apply to child sex offenders convicted prior to that date). The Act provided for:

- sex offenders to register with local police service

- sex offenders to register any change of address

- key responsibility on police to monitor compliance

The Criminal Justice Act 2003 revised this law and introduced a 'duty to cooperate' which was to involve MAPPAs working with a wider range of agencies. The legislation involves cooperation between police, prison and probation services to:

- establish arrangements for assessing and managing the risks posed by sexual and violent offenders

- review and monitor the arrangements

- publish an annual report on their operation

There are three categories of offenders:

1. Registered Sex Offenders (RSOs), that is those sexual offenders required to register under the terms of the Sex Offender Act (1997) and its amendments

2. Violent offenders and those sexual offenders who are not required to register

3. Any other offender who, because of the offences committed by them (wherever they have been committed) are considered to pose a risk of serious harm to the public.

The length of time offenders remain within the MAPPA is determined by:

- the length of their sex offender registration requirement (a minimum of five years)
- the length of the post-release supervision licence
- their continuing to pose risk of serious harm.

However, very few MAPPA offenders pose very high risks. It is upon the assessment of the risks of those few (the 'critical few') who pose the highest risks of causing serious harm or whose management is the most problematic that the MAPPA focuses.

The Multi-Agency Public Protection Panel

Membership
- Chair: Detective Chief Inspector
- Police Child Abuse Investigation Team / Police Community Service Unit
- Probation Service
- Prison Service
- Local Housing Authorities
- Local Education Authorities
- Youth Offending Team
- Local Authority Social Services
- NHS Trusts, Primary Care Trusts and Strategic Health Authorities
- Jobcentres Plus
- Registered social landlords which accommodate MAPPA offenders
- Electronic monitoring providers
- Two lay advisors appointed by the Home Office

Purpose
- To consider the current circumstances of registered sex offenders and dangerous or potentially dangerous adults in the community
- To develop a multi agency risk management strategy to
  - reduce the risk of further offending

- protect the public

Planning
- Cross-agency collation of information about adults in the community defined as a risk or potential risk to the public
- Targeted monitoring and surveillance
- Organisation of assessment and treatment
- Investigation and planning to safeguard possible victims
- Consideration and decision-making about community notification[1]

Records of meeting are only available to those attending and are not entered on client records. Referral to the MAPPP is through the appropriate agency representative.

---

1. Home Office Guidance 39/1997

YOUR ROLE IN CHILD PROTECTION: THE PROCEDURES

The importance of early recognition of child abuse

The importance of early recognition is that vulnerable children are identified at an early stage to try and prevent the continuance of abuse and the downward spiral into more dangerous situations for the child.

Children who slip through the child protection safety net, who suffer continued neglect, or emotional, physical and/or sexual abuse, are often children who become further vulnerable to abuse networks. Suspension from school, the breakdown of family support, running away from home, self harm and criminal behaviour are among factors which reinforce the self-perpetuating cycle of child abuse.

Children rarely lie about abuse

- Most children do not lie about abuse.
- Most children never tell
- Only 36% of survivors told as children[1]
- Many tell when they are older adults
- On average a child tells four adults before being 'heard'

---

1. NSPCC (1996), *Childhood Matters: National Commission of Inquiry into the Prevention of Child Abuse*, Vols 1 and 2. London, TSO

Barriers to making a referral

It is not difficult to make excuses to avoid referring a case of actual or suspected child abuse. Child abuse exists in a world of secrecy and silence and it is only by breaking that silence that children have a chance of being protected.

When you hear an allegation of abuse you take on yourself the child's pain and fear. It takes courage to activate the child protection process on behalf of the child. It's worth thinking about the factors which might prevent you taking that first step to breaking the abuse cycle.

Common reasons given as excuses for not referring include:

- fears of exposing the child to further abuse

- fears of breaking up the family

- fears of reprisals to yourself or your family

- fears of having to present evidence in court

- fears of misinterpreting or overreacting to the situation

- assuming another agency is dealing with the problem

- the 'rule of optimism' – convincing yourself everything will be all right

- assuming that one parent/carer will protect

- believing that the child is fantasising or lying

- being persuaded by a child's retraction of an allegation

- allowing a temporary improvement in the situation to distract you from the reality of the abuse

- feeling unable to comprehend the unbelievable nature of a disclosure

- experiencing the pain of abuse you yourself may have suffered

Remember that the information you have may only be a fragment of the full picture. If professionals, non-statutory workers and members of the public do not share their concerns about children, the full picture of abuse may never come to light.

Child abuse is a painful and difficult subject

All of us have been children and have taken those childhood experiences with us into adult life. Most of us have direct experience of being with or working with children of all ages. You will already have some valuable skills in being able to assess what is and what is not child abuse.

We must be able to address our own feelings and reactions to the subject if we are to hear what children are telling us about abuse and see child abuse when it confronts us. .

Some situations in child protection work can cause feelings such as depression, nausea, shaking, shock, coldness, anger, guilt. If we are overwhelmed and immobilised by these distressing feelings we will not be capable of responding appropriately to protect the child.

If we are to remain calm and be able to listen to the child we must put these genuine feelings to one side.

What is your role if a child discloses to you?

Specialist police officers and social workers are trained in the investigative interviewing of children. Although your own needs, understandably, will urge you to ask the child a lot of questions about the alleged abuse, this is not your role.

You may need to find out just enough about the alleged abuse in order to make a decision about the need for referral. If you need to ask the child questions or clarify what they are saying, make sure that you use open-ended questions. Should the case go to court you may be called as a witness and the court will need to be convinced that you have not contaminated the evidence by putting words or suggestions into the child's mind.

Examples of open-ended, non-leading questions:
- *Please tell me how it happened?*
- *Tell me more?*
- *Please explain that a bit further?*

If you are the first point of contact for a child wishing to disclose you are a very important person for that particular child. Many survivors of child abuse say that having the first person they told be supportive was the first step in recovering from their experience. Children often drip-feed information giving small clues over a period of time. Your supportive response at each stage will encourage the child to make further disclosure.

So what can you do?

- Tell the child that you take what they are saying very seriously

- Reassure the child that she/he is not to blame

- Let the child know that you understand how difficult it is to talk about such experiences and that she/he is brave to tell

- Be calm and reassuring

- Explain that you cannot promise to keep what the child tells you a secret

- Say that you take what they say very seriously and will involve a social worker/ police officer in order to work towards making the child safe and that you will continue to support them

- Don't make false promises / reassurances to the child which may not be able to be fulfilled

- Make accurate records

Remember . . .

It is important to preserve the innocence of the child and not to introduce abusive concepts to them. Corruption is when as professionals we introduce abusive concepts to the non-abused child.

Children commonly retract allegations of child abuse. A retraction does not discredit the original allegation but should raise questions about why the child has withdrawn the allegation.

It is *not* your role to physically examine a child. This is the role of the Child Protection Doctor or a medical expert appointed by them. If the child has marks which are easily visible then you should make a record of what you have seen. Do not look under a child's clothing to examine any injuries.

It is difficult to be definitive about whether or not it is acceptable to touch a child who is disclosing child abuse. To a child who has suffered abuse, any touch may have a very different meaning from that intended by the protective adult. Also, a child who has suffered abuse may not have an appropriate sense of boundaries or understand the need to keep themselves safe. It is important therefore to be cautious and to convey empathy through other means such as tone of voice, non-verbal behaviour or the use of toys.

Making accurate records

Written recording during the interview
It may be possible to write down phrases and words whilst the child is talking which can be used to trigger recall when the full recording is made. This should only be done if the child is in agreement and if it feels comfortable

Written recording immediately after the interview
It is very important to record exactly what the child said using the child's vocabulary even if the meaning is unclear

Recording your own responses
Your verbal and non-verbal responses should be recorded and it should be clear that a non-leading approach has been used.

Recording the context of the disclosure
The context in which a child chooses to tell about an incident of abuse can provide valuable information to the investigating team, e.g. the child was watching a particular video or was playing with dolls in the home corner

Recording the emotional context of the disclosure
The emotional context can provide valuable clues to the investigating team. A child may make serious statements in a joking way or may present as tearful and distressed. Children may speak about very serious matters in a matter of fact way which is surprising to adults.

Recording repetition
If a child repeats statements these should be recorded. Consistency in a child's repeated statements adds to the strength of the evidence.

How do you make a referral?

- Follow your organisation's internal guidelines reporting to your manager or supervisor as required.

- Your local child protection procedures will provide clear guidelines on how to make a referral to social services and police in your area.

- If medical attention is urgently required then refer directly to your local hospital.

- All referrals must be made to social services. Children and Families departments have a social worker on duty to respond to emergencies. There is always an out-of-hours team.

- The Police Child Abuse Investigation Team (CAIT) also has a police officer on duty at all times.

- You can refer anonymously but it is far better to provide your details so that further information may be sought. You can also call any of the agencies above for advice about referral.

Useful information about alleged perpetrators

Quite often in case of child abuse the police are asked to do a police check on an alleged perpetrator. This is more difficult than it seems, especially as the Police Child Abuse Investigation Team are often given only a name! The following information is helpful to police enquiries:

- Name (including middle names and aliases)
- Address / former address
- Telephone number / mobile phone number
- Date of birth
- Place of birth
- Ethnic origin
- Description (particularly height and distinguishing features)
- Employment / previous employment
- Car make / number
- Method of offending

What about informing the parents/carers?

The statutory agencies work in partnership with parents, communicating with them openly and honestly, but there are times when it is not in the best interests of the child for the parent to be informed before the child has been interviewed. Depending on your role within your agency you may wish to seek advice from the duty social worker before speaking with the parents. Remember that each case is unique and demands its own particular strategy. Be cautious about taking too much responsibility onto yourself.

What about informing other colleagues in your agency?

In child protection work information is shared on a 'need to know basis'. Certain information may need to be shared immediately in order to protect the child. Other decisions about sharing information are made at the strategy meeting.

What happens when you make a referral?

The social worker on duty will check if the child and family are known to social services. Following any other checks, for example with health and education, the social worker will liaise with the police officer on duty in the Child Abuse Investigation Team (CAIT), send through a police referral form and a strategy discussion will take place. The police will check their own records to see if the case is known to them.

If immediate action is necessary to protect the child such action will be taken. This may involve legal procedures and/or paediatric examinations. This is the exception and usually a strategy meeting is organised quickly so that the police officer and social worker can meet with the person who made the referral or with any other professional who has relevant knowledge about the child and family. When a medical examination may be needed, a senior doctor should be included in the discussion.

The strategy meeting

It may not be your role to be involved in this stage of child protection procedures, but it is important to understand the processes.

A strategy meeting is a professionals-only meeting convened by social services and chaired by a team manager. Parents and young people do not attend. The purpose of the meeting is to:

- share information and allow professional debate and analysis

- decide whether Section 47 inquiries should be initiated or continued if they have already begun

- plan how enquiries should be handled, including the need for medical treatment and by whom

- agree what action is needed immediately to safeguard the child and/or provide interim services and support

- determine what information about the strategy discussion will be shared with the family unless such sharing may place a child at risk of significant harm or jeopardise police investigations into any alleged offences

You may find that from this stage you feel a bit left out of the process and are wondering what is happening. Social workers and police officers are extremely busy people and will be preoccupied with the protection of the child. Don't be afraid to keep in touch with them.

Assessment

"the aim of assessment is to guide action. Assessment is an activity in itself and a process of understanding. Without it workers are left to react to events and intervene in an unplanned way."

DoH (2000), Framework of Assessment for
Children in Need and their Families

It is very important *not* to confuse assessment and investigation. These are two separate but connected processes. An assessment of the child and family will commonly inform an investigation under Section 47 of the Children Act 1989 but does not replace it. An investigation is conducted jointly between social workers and police and considers risk posed by perpetrators and alleged perpetrators.

Assessments:

- are child centred

- are rooted in child development

- are ecological in their approach

- ensure equality of opportunity

- require work in partnership with children and families

- build on strengths as well as identify weaknesses

- are multi-agency in their approach to assessment and the provision of services

- are a continuing process, not a single event

- are carried out in parallel with other action and providing services

- are grounded in evidence-based knowledge

Investigation

It is important to remember that assessment is only one aspect of an investigation under Section 47 of the Children Act 1989. Assessment informs the investigation and does not replace it. An initial assessment (seven days) should not prevent urgent action being taken to protect a child should that be required, for instance a Section 47 beginning or immediate consultation with the police if the child falls within that criteria.

Social services have a legal duty to investigate any situation where there are concerns about the welfare of a child or young person (up to the age of 18 years). The investigation focuses on the safety of the child. Even anonymous referrals must be investigated.

The process of investigation

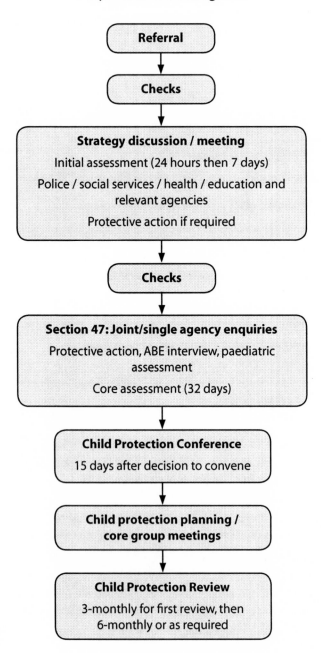

Referral

Checks

Strategy discussion / meeting

Initial assessment (24 hours then 7 days)

Police / social services / health / education and relevant agencies

Protective action if required

Checks

Section 47: Joint/single agency enquiries

Protective action, ABE interview, paediatric assessment

Core assessment (32 days)

Child Protection Conference

15 days after decision to convene

Child protection planning / core group meetings

Child Protection Review

3-monthly for first review, then 6-monthly or as required

Referrals from neighbours, friends and relatives or members of the public who know the family and child must be investigated fully.

An investigation will usually involve the following:

- talking to the person who has expressed concern

- talking to the child

- talking to the parents or carers of the child

- liaising with other agencies which have knowledge about the child/family

- seeking specialist advice where necessary to find out about the child's ethnic origin, religion, language or disability and using interpreters where necessary

- assessing the ability of the non-abusive carer/parent to protect the child

In cases where an offence may have been committed, the child and parents may be interviewed by the police or the child may be interviewed in a video suite by specially trained social workers and police officers.

A child may need to be looked after by relatives, foster carers or a residential care unit whilst an investigation takes place and plans for the child's future are being agreed. Usually the placement of a child outside the family is agreed with the parents and the child is 'accommodated' in partnership with the parents. Sometimes when there is conflict between the parents and the social services a court order may be sought to safeguard the protection of the child in safe place.

Child Protection Conferences

If a decision is made to convene a Child Protection Conference this will involve all the key people involved with the child and family. It is usually chaired by an independent social worker. The parents are invited and meet the chairperson before the conference.

The aim of a conference is:

- to bring together and analyse in an inter-agency setting the information which has been obtained about the child's health, development and functioning, and the parent's or carer's capacity to ensure the child's safety and promote the child's health and development

- to make judgments about the likelihood of a child suffering significant harm in the future

- to decide that future action is needed to safeguard and promote his or her welfare, how that action will be taken forward and with what intended outcomes

Requirements of registration

Even if the child has been injured or abused, no child's name may be placed on the Child Protection Register unless there are continuing protection issues.

The conference must always be satisfied that at least one of the following conditions is met:

1. There are one or more specifically identifiable incidents which can be described as adversely affecting the child. These may be acts of commission or omission, and may be physical, sexual, emotional or neglectful. Professional judgement must be that further incidents are likely.

2. Although there have been no specifically identifiable incidents, significant harm is expected on the basis of:
   - professional judgement of findings of the investigation leading to the conference
   - research evidence

The conference must also establish, as far as possible, the cause of harm or likelihood of harm and consider whether other children in the household satisfy the criteria for registration.

Interpretation of the criteria must take account of the child and family's cultural and linguistic background, ethnic origin and religious persuasion., as well as issues relating to gender, disability, class and sexual preference. If the case conference decides that the criteria for registration are satisfied, it must decide in which category or categories the child's name will be registered, i.e. physical abuse, emotional abuse, sexual abuse or neglect.

The key worker

If a child's name is placed on the Register under one or more of the categories of abuse a key worker is appointed. The key worker:

- is responsible for making sure that the outline child protection plan is developed into a more detailed inter-agency plan.

- should complete the core assessment of the child and family, securing contributions from Core Group members and others as necessary.

- is also responsible for acting as lead worker for the inter-agency work with the child and family.

- should co-ordinate the contribution of family members and other agencies to planning the actions which need to be taken, putting the child protection plan into effect, and reviewing progress against the objectives set out in the plan.

All the professionals involved in the Child Protection Plan must keep the key worker informed about the child's wellbeing.

The core group

A core group is identified which includes the key professionals involved in the Child Protection Plan. All members of the core group are jointly responsible for the formulation and implementation of the child protection plan as a detailed working tool, refining the plan as needed and monitoring progress against specified objectives as defined at the initial child protection conference.

- Membership
  - Key worker – takes the lead
  - Child – if appropriate
  - Family
  - Professionals and foster carers with direct contact with the family
- First meeting within 10 days of the initial conference
- Record of meetings to include record of agreed action

Child Protection Plan

The purpose of the Child Protection Plan is to:
- identify risk of significant harm to the child and ways in which the child can be protected through an inter-agency plan based on assessment and investigation findings
- establish short-term and longer term aims and objectives that are clearly linked to reducing the risk of harm to the child and promoting the child's welfare
- be clear about who will have responsibility for what actions – including action by family members – within what specified timescales
- outline ways of monitoring and evaluating the progress of the plan

Child Protection Reviews

The first Child Protection Review is held three months after the conference and subsequently at six month intervals. As soon as the professionals are sure that the situation has improved for the child and that there is no longer a need for a protection plan, the review will move towards deregistration.

Paediatric assessment

It is very important that children are not examined by doctors more than is absolutely necessary. It is quite common to offer a child a paediatric consultation rather than an examination so that they can ask any questions themselves.

All referrals for paediatric assessments are made to the child protection doctor on duty who decides which doctor is the most appropriate to see the child. For the examination of a bruise the child may be taken to a general practitioner, whereas for a sexual abuse case there may be a need for the child to be examined by a forensic medical examiner and a consultant paediatrician.

Consent for examination

- No child may be examined without the child's consent except in a life-saving emergency

- The child must be of sufficient age and understanding to make an informed decision

- Examination without consent may be held in law to be an assault

The child interview

A young person may be formally interviewed on video by a police officer and social worker, usually in a child interview suite. *Achieving Best Evidence in criminal proceedings for vulnerable and intimidated witnesses including children*[1] provides detailed guidance about how children should be interviewed in a child-centred way using a phased interview approach. The child is given time to provide their own free narrative account of events prior to the use of open questioning by the interviewers. They must

---

1. Home Office (2002)

consent to the interview process and must be capable of undergoing cross examination in court should the case go forward to criminal proceedings.

What help can be given to parents?

Wherever possible parents are supported in providing the proper care for their children. Apart from the involvement of the social worker, GP, health visitor, and school staff, families may be offered resources such as nursery places for their younger children to relieve stress on the family and to offer the children learning opportunities.

At Family Centres parents gain the opportunity to learn parenting skills and sometimes Family Support Workers go into the home and advice the family about the care of the children and management of the home environment.

Some parents may receive support from the Mental Health Service if there is mental illness in the family. Parents who have themselves suffered abuse as children may make use of counselling services or gain strength and insight from joining a survivors' group. Sometimes respite care is provided by child-minders or foster-carers to relieve stress on the family.

With the co-operation between the family and the professionals, children are most frequently protected within their own homes. Among the non-statutory organisations which support families are Homestart and Relate.

GOOD PRACTICE IN CHILD PROTECTION

Involving children and young people in the child protection process

Older children are invited to attend Child Protection Conferences and reviews. Professionals must listen to the child's views on their protection needs and report this to the conference. Their views may be expressed through drawings, writing or audio/video recordings.

It is essential that every effort is made to bring the child's views into the meeting as well as direct observations about the child's welfare from safe adults close to the child.

There are many useful tools to assist in obtaining the child's view, some of which are listed below. Full references are given at the back of this resource book.

Turning Points (NSPCC)

A resource pack for communicating with children – has a wealth of resources for direct work with children and young people

Once Upon a Time: Therapeutic stories (N Davis)

This is an excellent resource providing healing stories for reading to children in all situations and not requiring interpretation.

My Body My Book (A Peake & K Rouf)

This provides a useful opportunity for children to talk about safe and unsafe touch.

The Anti-Colouring Book (S Striker & E Kimmel)

This book of pictures for children to complete can be adapted for use in relation to many different situations and investigations. The pictures allow the child to express feelings and thoughts undirected by adults.

Communicating with children

Communication with children who have been damaged – physically mentally, emotionally – as a result of child abuse is a daunting task. As adults we have often been distanced and estranged from the world of small children. Re-entering this world requires us to establish a contact with our own inner child, and draw on our creative and imaginative resources. Many of us have simply forgotten how to use these skills, though they are present in us all as we were all children once. With our adult need to direct and control, we impose formal settings and structures on children and expect them to enter our world and relate to us on our terms. We use a flow of words and do not understand when the child clams up and avoids our gaze. We raise our voices, plead, cajole but recognise that this impedes communication even further. We feel flustered, stuck, awkward, embarrassed. An uncommunicative child is an absolute enigma, for even the most persistent adult.

Rather than expecting children to enter our world, Madge Bray suggests that we consider turning the whole process about. My own image for this is that if we wish to make contact with a child we must first, like Alice, be prepared to shrink in size in order to enter the world as they experience it. We must allow ourselves to interact at the child's level, rather than the level we are accustomed to as adults.

When we enter this world we may find things which deeply disturb us. A child having sexual knowledge and experience clashes sharply with our belief in childhood innocence and our emotions are likely to be those of shock, horror and disgust. The discovery may make us want to beat a hasty retreat and slam the door shut. Madge Bray asks us to stay a little longer, "to be willing to explore this world with the child and not let our own fears hold us back… we need to re-appraise our approach to abused children so that we may become more ready to learn from what they tell us."[1]

Remember …

- Be aware of using age-appropriate language
- Don't overwhelm the child
- Keep it simple
- Allow silences
- Respond to non-verbal behaviour
- Think how the child is perceiving you and your role
- Be aware of your own agendas
- What control does the child have in the interaction
- Don't introduce abuse concepts to the child
- Consider gender, ethnic origin and cultural issues
- Avoid interpreting what the child is saying
- Hear difficult and painful statements
- Don't put words in the child's mouth
- Don't assume abuse has occurred

Working in partnership with parents

The overarching principle of the Children Act 2004 is acting in the best interests of the child. Those working together to safeguard children should agree a common understanding in each case and at each stage of the work about how children and families will be involved in the child protection processes and what information is shared with them. There should be a presumption of openness and joint decision-making, and a willingness to listen to families and capitalise on their strengths.

In particular, those working in child protection should:

- treat families with dignity and respect

---

1. Bray, M (1997)

- ensure family members' rights to a courteous, professional competent service while understanding the child's welfare is paramount

- bearing in mind the need to safeguard the child, do not invade privacy more than is necessary

- be clear about power and authority and the purpose of intervention

- be aware of the impact on the family of this power and the implications of intervention

- respect confidentiality

- listen to the concerns of children and families

- consider children within their family, community , religious and cultural context

- consider the strengths and potential of family members as well as their weaknesses

- ensure families know their rights to services and to refuse services

- use plain, jargon-free language

- be open and honest about concerns

- allow time for understanding (balanced with the immediate needs of the child for safety)

- distinguish between personal feelings, values, prejudices, beliefs and professional roles and responsibilities

- acknowledge any distress caused to the family through interventions[1]

1. DoH (1995), *The Challenge of Partnership in Child Protection*

Parents' views about Child Protection Conferences

The following quotes are taken from a 1997 book, *Strong Mothers: A resource for mothers of children who have been sexually assaulted.*[1]

- "They decided they would put her name on the Register. It was the end of the world for me. I couldn't understand why they'd done it. I know now that it was because they were not sure who the abuser was. I felt stupid and undermined."

- "They asked me if she had any health problems and I said 'No'. Then the Chair looked at my doctor and said. 'Has she?' I thought, 'Well why the fuck ask me?'"

- "I wish I'd kept all the letters they sent me after the conference because it said my daughter should have counselling and she never got any."

- "Things were brought up about my husband's past which I didn't know. I think he should have been notified that this would be done, so he had the chance to tell me first."

- "When we got there and went into the room, I was amazed at the size of the table. I thought I hope they don't fill all these chairs. They did."

- "I could feel they had power and I had none."

- "We had to introduce ourselves and I was asked to go first. I messed it up. I couldn't say my name and who I was. That finished it. I didn't come in with much confidence but after that I felt really stupid."

- "I didn't know all the people. A teacher was there who would be her head teacher when she went on to secondary school"

- "It was difficult to keep track of what was happening. I felt everything was pushing in on me."

---

1. Peake, A, & Fletcher, M (1997)

- "I said what I thought they wanted to hear because I was frightened to death they'd take my children away."

- "I felt I had to play ball."

- "No one asked me how I was going to get home."

- "No-one can blame you more than you blame yourself. When someone says something about you it confirms all the bad things you think about yourself."

- "I'd been a playgroup worker so I had always been on the other side before. It was very difficult."

Working with the non-abusive parent/carer

Parents whose children have suffered abuse are likely to go through emotional stages comparable to those commonly experienced during bereavement. Initially they may feel shock and disbelief leading professionals to think that the parent is being uncooperative or unsupportive of their child. It is important to be patient and support the parent towards an acceptance of what has happened.

The following emotional responses are common – the list has been compiled by non-abusive parents/carers.

- Loss of trust in others
- Disbelief
- Torn loyalties
- Shock
- Guilt
- Anger towards the abuser
- Anger towards the child
- Pain / depression
- Feeling alone and isolated
- Grief

- 'My family is no longer normal'
- 'This sort of thing doesn't happen in my family'
- Loss of trust in own judgement
- Shame
- Numbness
- Memories of own experience of abuse

There are many reasons why a parent/carer may not have known about the abuse their child was suffering.

- The abuser is usually someone known to the parent and in a position of trust and responsibility – they are the last person the parent would suspect. They may have a wife and family or be a respected person within the community leading the parent to be disbelieving about the person's capacity to abuse children.

- The abuser often manipulates the parent / child relationship to undermine any closeness between them. The abuser may destroy the parent's sense of self esteem and confidence in parenting.

- The abuser will go to great lengths to demonstrate his/her concern for the child (buying gifts, taking them out etc.) which can deceive the vulnerable parent.

- Children find it extremely difficult to disclose the abuse to their parent, they may be threatened by the abuser or feel guilty or ashamed about the abuse. They may fear their parents' response or the break-up of their family.

- Even when a child shows signs of being abused, the child or the abuser will give the parent many other plausible explanations for these – e.g. behavioural problems at school or illnesses. The parent loses trust in his/her own judgement.

- The abuser may have targeted the child because of family instability which makes it more difficult for the child to gain protection from the parents.

- The abuser will be so cunning that child sexual abuse will be very difficult for a parent to detect. Children have spoken of being sexually abused in the living room whilst the parents are present watching television and unaware of what was happening to their child.

- The parent may live with a violent partner and be afraid to speak out or to acknowledge the abuse of their child.

- Parents want to believe their children are safe and that they have brought them up in the right way so that abuse would not happen to them.

Responding to the needs of refugee and asylum-seeking families

When child protection assessments are made of refugee families a number of factors need consideration:

- It may be difficult for professionals trying to assist as immigration law commonly takes precedence over the Children Acts 1989 and 2004. Advice should be sought from some of the specialist organisations listed in the Further Resources at the back of this book.

- It is important to question the family's perception of the role of professionals in protecting children. Depending on their past experiences, parents may perceive police involvement as repressive.

- The child's statement or demonstration of abuse may be confused with sexual and physical violence they have experienced or witnessed in their country of origin. Parents must be asked about their experiences in order to place the child's view in perspective, remembering that they may themselves have 'blocked out' some experiences as a result of trauma.

- Parents' reactions and their ability to parent effectively must be assessed in the context of their experiences. They may well be suffering Post Traumatic Stress Syndrome, in which case referral to specialist agencies may be helpful. Children may require specialist psychotherapy.

- The impact of family insecurity as a result of current legal status must be considered.

- Parental non-cooperation must be evaluated in the context of past and current experience of authorities and potential inability to confront the pain of past experiences.

Anti-oppressive practice in child protection

Professional responses to families must take into account power differentials and the structures which puts minority service users in an inferior or submissive position.

majority	minority
white	black
non-disabled	disabled
Christian	other religion
middle/upper class	working class
English language	other languages
heterosexual	gay/lesbian

Think of 'adult / child' in this context . 'Childism' is the oppression of children.

All current legislation relating to the protection of children stresses the importance of paying due attention to the racial, cultural, religious and linguistic background of the child. But what does this really mean?

If a child or family's first language is not English then an interpreter must be sought and fully involved in case planning. But the availability of good interpreting is not enough!

How do professionals gain an understanding of cultural and religious issues in child protection? How do they decide whether a parent deliberately set out to harm a child or whether they were carrying out a culturally accepted practice?

If this practice causes significant harm to the child then even if it is accepted within a particular cultural group social services has a duty to intervene and investigate with sensitivity. Professionals must seek expert advice. This is available through contact with community ethnic minority groups, and through specialist resources.

PROFESSIONAL ISSUES

Professional dangerousness

Professional dangerousness is the process by which individual workers or multi-disciplinary networks can, usually unwittingly, act in such a way as to collude with, maintain or increase the dangerous dynamics of the family in which abuse takes place.

Here are some key examples of professional dangerousness.

1. **Rule of optimism**
   Professionals tend to want to believe that all is well for the child. Even when the indicators of abuse are visible there is tendency to explain them away and be convinced that the child is safe. This is a form of denial and probably the most common form of dangerous practice.

2. **The Stockholm syndrome**
   This is based on situations where hostages begin to identify with the cause of their captors. It is a survival mechanism common in child abuse cases. Sometimes a parent or abuser is powerful and intimidating and the worker will begin to see the adult's point of view rather than the child's.

3. **Professional accommodation syndrome**
   The worker may mirror the child's retraction of abuse, deny the reality of the abuse and be keen to be persuaded that any allegation by the child must be suppressed. Any other possible reason for the abuse will tend to become accepted in preference to the possibility that abuse has occurred.

4. **Exaggeration of hierarchy**
   Adults of low status who report abuse may not be heard or taken seriously even though they may be close to the child,

e.g. neighbours, friends or a nursery worker. A psychiatrist, lawyer or paediatrician will probably get their important opinions heard more readily by other professionals.

5. **Concrete solutions**
Professionals respond swiftly to abuse situations with practical solutions such as housing, washing machines, or money rather than by investigating the alleged abuse.

6. **Assessment paralysis**
Sometimes professionals feel helpless and incapacitated. It might be thought that change is hard to achieve because the family have always lived in an abusive way and it is just their way of life.

7. **Stereotyping**
Professionals may make assumptions about how families bring up their children. These may include cultural stereotypes, examples of which are given in the next section.

8. **False compliance**
Parents may be able to convince professionals that they are cooperating to protect the child while in fact this is no the case. Professionals may become so enmeshed with the family that they do not see the needs of the child.

9. **Omnipotence**
Professionals believe that they know the best interests of the child and will not revisit their perceptions in the light of new evidence.

10. **Closure**
Families may shut out professionals. Calls go unanswered, appointments are missed, curtains are closed and doors locked. This dynamic may be mirrored by professionals avoiding contact with the family.

11. **Role confusion**
Professionals may be unclear about tasks and assume that someone else is responsible for protecting the child. In child

protection *everyone* has 'prime responsibility' for the safety of
the child.

12. Children unheard

Every inquiry highlights the central importance of listening to
the child. Although children do find it hard to speak of abuse
it has been shown that prior to a child's tragic death they have
often forewarned someone in authority about the risk.

13. Priority given to recent information

Information which is recent, emotional, and vivid takes
precedence over the old. Inquiries inevitably demonstrate
that there was among agencies a great deal of knowledge and
understanding about actual or potential harm to the child. New
information must be examined in the context of prior facts.

14. Non-compliance with statutory procedures

Inquiries commonly report that legislation, policy and practice
are sound but that professionals did not comply with their
implementation. When child protection procedures are in
place such as conferences and strategy meetings, children
generally become safe.

False cultural assumptions

There are many false assumptions which may pervade child
protection practice and contribute to professional dangerousness.

For instance, it is common belief that families of African-
Caribbean origin beat their children or that incest occurs commonly
in families of Irish origin. In fact all forms of abuse occur in all
cultures and there is no evidence to suggest that any aspect of the
abuse of children happens more in a particular ethnic minority
group.

Sometimes assumptions lead to false beliefs that a child is being
protected. For example, in the Tyra Henry case, the belief in the

strong, coping African-Caribbean grandmother prevented professionals listening to her distress.[1]

Women of Asian origin are often perceived as fragile and subor-
dinate; men of African origin are caricatured as aggressive; middle-
class white UK families are assumed to be giving their children
the best of care; etc. All these assumptions are dangerous in child
protection work.

Assessments made against the background of a Eurocentric
model of child care may lead to an over-critical approach and
punitive intervention and controls placed on the family based on
ignorance and/or discrimination.

However, a too liberal approach by white professionals can
lead to abuse within ethnic minority families being overlooked or
dismissed. For example, a mentally ill mother who neglects her
children and is reported by white neighbours might be perceived
as a victim of racial harassment and the abuse of the children
overlooked. In another case an allegation of abuse may in fact be
malicious and the result of racial harassment. These factors must be
considered as part of an investigation.

Sometimes ethnic minority families make decisions in ways
which professionals need to understand, making reference for
instance to the elders in the extended family or religious group.

Working together in this context means crossing cultural
boundaries and helping each other understand, in order to establish
a reliable safety net for the ethnic minority child and family.

Taking the child's voice forward: personal commitment and whistleblowing

It can be very demanding to challenge individuals, organisations
or processes that you feel may be putting children at risk of sig-

---

1. London Borough of Lambeth (1987)

nificant harm. It is important to consider the professional implications of taking the child's voice forward and consider how far
you personally would be prepared to go to ensure a child's safety.
Remember that the dictionary definition of safeguarding is:

- Protection
- Security
- Safe-keeping
- Security from danger
- Being protected against hurt or injury

When the community police officer in Gloucester was walking
down the street and heard the children in Cromwell Street speaking
of terrible and bizarre things going on in the cellar of Fred and Rose
West, he was open to hearing the children. He told his manager
who told social services and the investigation began. If at any point
someone had dismissed the comments as just the whim of street
children the terrible murders and sexual exploitation would have
continued unchallenged.[1]

But children who disclose abuse are commonly met with denial
and disbelief. And those professionals who hear their cry for help
may also be met with similar responses. There have been a number
of large-scale investigations into child abuse where the professionals who tried to protect the children became scapegoated and
defined as 'over zealous' or ' obsessional'. The professional voices,
and therefore the children's voices, were thus discredited.

Alison Taylor worked as a residential social worker in North Wales
children's homes and exposed the serious abuse of children. For 15
years she raised her concerns and was not heard. She stated that:

"200 years ago Beethoven denounced a priest for abusing boys
in Vienna and was widely condemned for doing so. Nothing
changes. I am repeatedly accused of canvassing for allegations,

---

1. For a summary of the West case visit www.bbc.co.uk/crime/caseclosed/
fredwest1.shtml

manipulating children's antipathy towards carers, exaggerating small reprimands into abuses and even organising a nationwide conspiracy of false allegations for gain."

In 1999 the Public Interest Disclosure Act was implemented and provided some protection for adults who blow the whistle about injustice. However the law is complicated and if you find yourself in a situation where in any way you are prevented from doing the job you are paid to do as a protector of children you may wish to contact Public Concern at Work (www.pcaw.co.uk), an organisation which provides support and legal advice, or Freedom to Care (www.ftc.co.uk).

You need to consider what safeguards to put in place for yourself. You might join a professional organisation or trade union which provides advice and legal indemnity. It is generally the case that a disclosure will not be defined as reasonable unless all routes for reporting the matter through the usual channels have been exhausted. The Local Safeguarding Children's Board would be central to anyone wishing to raise such important matters about children's safety. CSCI (Commission for Social Care Inspection) inspectors may also be contacted with concerns – see www.csci.gov.uk.

Child abuse and child protection: how do we cope?

"Child abuse presents a powerful challenge to society, in the face of which its major defence mechanisms have been denial and minimisation. Those who work in this field do not expect it to be pain free but nor do they expect or have spare resources to deal with that same denial and minimisation of their feelings and needs when this is mirrored within their own workplace . . . Powerless professionals cannot protect children."[1]

1. Morrison, T (2001) *Staff Supervision in Social Care.* Brighton, Pavilion

It is not unusual for professionals and non-statutory workers to feel contaminated by the subject of child abuse. Sometimes one or two particular details of a case stay with us to haunt us even when the case is over. Even people who have worked in this field for years find themselves taken aback by the details of a new case.

It is important to seek help for yourself if the work has affected you. It may be that learning about or dealing with child abuse has raised personal issues for you or triggered memories about your own experiences. Please seek help and advice. There are details of counselling organisations at the back of this book and most agencies have their own counselling schemes for staff. Don't avoid the feelings and hope they will go away. It is always advisable to seek help.

What if you have reported a case and you feel that you are left carrying the responsibility inappropriately? We tell the child to find another trusted adult if they are not heard – surely the same rule applies to adults too? There are child protection advisors in health and social services who are always willing to help you think through what has happened to the referral you made. The Police Child Abuse Investigation Team officers are always willing to give advice.

Why don't you identify a trusted colleague with whom you can share how you feel about a particular case – obviously with due regard for confidentiality and protecting the details of the child and family.

Survival skills

This list is reproduced from *Staff Supervision in Social Care* by Tony Morrison[1]

- To know who I am and why I am doing this work
- To develop good self awareness
- To recognise that some clients will not change

---

1. Morrison (2001)

- To develop realistic expectations of myself, my colleagues and my managers

- To be clear as to the limits of my personal responsibility

- To be clear about the issues of authority and control

- To accept that a healthy scepticism is not uncaring

- To know when I need help, how to ask for it and who from

- To demand good supervision

- To maintain a strong leisure life

- To give myself permission to learn from mistakes, be unsure, have feelings and celebrate what I am good at

- To believe that I do not have to be stressed or victimised to care

Relevant articles/books

- The Care Standards Tribunal website (www.carestand-ardstribunal.org.uk) has the decision on the case of Lisa Arthurworrey *v* Secretary of State (the social worker for Victoria Climbié). The judge upheld that child protection work is a complex and specialist task and that Lisa was inexperienced, untrained, had a high workload and poor supervision, and worked to flawed policies.

- Munro, E. (2005) 'A Systems Approach to Investigating Child Abuse Deaths' in *British Journal of Social Work*, Vol.35;4, pp531-546

- Cairns, K (1999) *Surviving Paedophilia: Traumatic stress after organised and network child sexual abuse.* Gloucestershire, Akamas

- Jones, C (2001) 'Voices from the front line: State social workers and new Labour' in *British Journal of Social Work*, Vol.1:31, pp547-62

FURTHER RESOURCES

Quiz answers

True: 3, 4, 7, 9, 12, 14, 16, 17, 20, 21, 29, 31, 34, 40

Reading list

The titles in **bold** are particularly relevant and include survivors' accounts.

Abrahams, C (1994) *The Hidden Victims: Children and domestic violence.* London, NCH

Adcock, M & White, R (ed) (1998) *Significant Harm: Its management and outcome.* London, Significant Publications

Adie, K (2006) *Nobody's Child.* London, Hodder

Ayre, P and Barrett, D (2000) 'Young People and Prostitution: An end to the beginning', in *Children & Society Journal*, Vol.14 pp48-59

Barnardo's (2002) *Bitter Legacy: The emotional effects of domestic violence on children.* London, Barnardo's

Barrett, D (ed) (1997) *Child Prostitution in Britain: Dilemmas and practical responses.* London, The Children's Society

Barter, C (2001) 'Protecting Children from Racism and Racial Abuse', at www.nspcc.org.uk/inform/research/summariesinword

Batmanghelidjh, C (2006) *Shattered Lives: Children who live with courage and dignity.* London, Jessica Kingsley

Benn, H (2002) 'Multi-Agency Public Protection Arrangements', at www.mappaonline.co.uk

Biehal, N and Wade, W (2002) *Children Who Go Missing: Research, policy and practice.* London, Department of Health

Bichard Inquiry Report (2004). London, TSO [also available at www.bichardinquiry.org.uk]

Bray, M (1998) *Poppies on the Rubbish Heap: Sexual abuse – the child's voice.* **London, Jessica Kingsley**

Bridge Child Care Development Service & Gloucester SSD (1996) *'In Care Contacts' – The West Case: The report of a review of over 2000 files of young people in residential care.* London, The Bridge

Bridge Child Care Development Service & Islington ACPC (1990) *Neglect: A 50 year search for answers.* London, The Bridge

Bridge Child Care Development Service (1996) *Listening to Children: The issues.* London, The Bridge

Bridge Child Care Development Service (1995) *Paul: Death from neglect.* London, Islington ACPC

Bridge Child Care Development Service (1991) *Sukina: An evaluation of the circumstances leading to her death.* London, The Bridge

Briscoe, C (2006) *Ugly: The story of a loveless childhood.* **London, Hodder and Stoughton**

Cairns, K (2002) Attachment, Trauma and Resilience: Therapeutic Caring for Children. London, BAAF

Cairns, K (1999) *Surviving Paedophilia - Traumatic stress after organised and network child sexual abuse.* **Gloucestershire, Akamas**

Calder, M and Hackett, S (2003) *Assessment in Child Care.* Dorset, Russell House Publishing

Calder, M (1999) *Assessing Risk in Adult Males who Sexually Abuse Children.* Dorset, Russell House Publishing

Calder, M (2004) *Children Living with Domestic Violence: Towards a framework for assessment and intervention.* **Dorset, Russell House Publilshing**

Calder, M (1997) *Juveniles and Children who Sexually Abuse: A guide to risk assessment.* Dorset, Russell House Publishing:

ChildLine (1997) *Beyond the Limit: Children who live with parental alcohol misuse.* London, ChildLine

Children Act (1989). London, HMSO

Children Act (2004). London, TSO

Children's Society (1999) *Still Running: Children on the streets in the UK.* London, The Children's Society

CSCI (2005) *Safeguarding Children: The second Joint Chief Inspector's Report.* Newcastle, CSCI

Cleaver, H Unell and Aldgate, J (1999) *Children's Needs – Parenting Capacity: The impact of mental illness, problem alcohol and drug use and domestic violence on children's development*. London, TSO

Corby, B (2003) *Child Abuse: Towards a knowledge base*. Berkshire, OUP

Cross, M (2001) *Proud Child Safe Child: A Handbook for parents and carers of disabled children*. London, The Women's Press

D'Arcy, M and Gosling, P (1998) *Abuse of Trust: Frank Beck and the Leicestershire children's home scandal*. Oxford, Bowerdean Publishing

Davis, N (1999) Once Upon a Time: Therapeutic stories to heal abused children. Psychological Associates

Department for Education and Skills (2003) *Every Child Matters*. London, TS) [also available at www.everychildmatters.gov.uk]

Department for Education and Skills (2003) *Keeping Children Safe: The government's response to the Victoria Climbié Inquiry Report and the Joint Chief Inspectors Report*. London, TSO

Department for Education and Skills (2006) *Working Together to Safeguard Children: A guide for inter-agency working to safeguard and promote the welfare of children*. London, TSO [also available at www.everychildmatters.gov.uk/socialcare/safeguarding/ workingtogether/]

Department of Health (1991) *Child Abuse – A Study of Inquiry reports 1980-9: Review of 19 reports during the 80's*. London, HMSO

Department of Health (1995) *Child Protection: Messages from research*. London, HMSO

Department of Health (2002) *Children's Homes: National Minimum Standards*. London,TSO

Department of Health (2000) *Framework for the Assessment of Children in Need and their Families*. London, TSO http://www.dfes.gov. uk/qualityprotects

Department of Health (1998) *People Like Us: The review of the safeguards for children living away from home*. London, TSO

Department of Health (1995) *The Challenge of Partnership in Child Protection: A practice guide*. London,HMSO

Department of Health (2002) *Learning from Past Experience. A review of Serious Case Reviews*. London, TSO [also available at www.doh.gov. uk/qualityprotects]

Department of Health (2002) *Children Missing from Care and from Home: A guide to good practice*. London, TSO

Department of Health (2003) *National Plan for Safeguarding Children from Commercial Exploitation*. London, TSO

Department of Health (1999) *Safeguarding Children Involved in Prostitution: Working together to safeguard children*. **London,TSO.**

Department of Health (2001) *Safeguarding Children in Whom Illness is Induced or Fabricated by Carers*. **London, TSO.**

Dorkenoo, E (1995) *Cutting the Rose: Female genital mutilation – the practice and its prevention*. London, Minority Rights Publications

Falkov, A (1996) *A study of Working Together Part 8 Reports: Fatal child abuse and parental psychiatric disorder*. London, Department of Health

Fever, F (1997) *Who Cares?: Memories of a childhood in Barnardo's*. Hertfordshire, Time Warner Books

Fitzgerald, J (1998) 'Policy and Practice in Child Protection: Its relation to dangerousness', in *Dangerous Care: BridgeAlert Training Pack*. London, The Bridge

Foreign and Commonwealth Office et al (2004) *Young People and Vulnerable Adults Facing Forced Marriage: Practice guidance for social workers*. London, TSO [also available at www.adss.org.uk/publications/guidance/marriage.pdf]

Frampton, P (2004) *Golly in the Cupboard*. **Manchester, Tamic**

Greater London Authority (2004) *Making London Better for All Children and Young People*. London, Greater London Authority

Harbert, W (2005) *Bent Twigs*. London, Blackie and Co

Hare, B (2006) *Urban Grimshaw and the Shed Crew*. **London Sceptre**

Hester, M et al (2000) *Making an Impact: Children and domestic violence*. *London*, Whiting and Birch

Hillingdon Area Review Committee (1986) *Heidi Koseda*. London, London Borough of Hillingdon

Home Office (2002) *Achieving Best Evidence: Guidance for vulnerable or intimidated witnesses including children*. London, TSO [also available at www.cps.gov.uk]

Home Office (2002) *Protecting the Public: Strengthening protection against sex offenders and reforming the law of sexual offences*. London, TSO.

Home Office and Department of Health (2002) *Complex Child Abuse Investigation: Inter agency issues.* London,Home Office

Horton, C (2005) *Working with Children: Facts, figures and information 2006-7*. London, Atlantic Books

Howarth, J (ed) (2000) *The Child's World: Assessing children in need.* London, Department of Health

Howe, D (2005) *Child Abuse and Neglect: Attachment, development and intervention.* Basingstoke, Palgrave Macmillan

Howells, J (1974) *Remember Maria.* Surrey, Butterworths

Hughes, M, Downie, A and Sharma, N (2000) *Counting the Cost of Child Poverty.* London, Barnardo's

Humphreys, M (1996) *Empty Cradles*. London, Corgi

Hunt, G (ed) (1998) *Whistleblowing in the Social Services.* London, Hodder Arnold

Jones, D (2003) Communicating with Vulnerable Children. London, Gaskell (Royal College of Psychiatrists)

Kane, J (1998) *Sold for Sex.* London, Arena

Levy, A (1993) *The Pindown Inquiry.* London, HMSO

Lew, M (1990) *Victims No Longer: A guide for men recovering from sexual child abuse.* London, Perenniel

Lockhat, H (2004) *Female Genital Mutilation: Treating the tears.* Middlesex, Middlesex University Press.

London Borough of Brent (1985) *A Child in Trust: The report of the Inquiry into the death of Jasmine Beckford.* London, London Borough of Brent

London Borough of Greenwich (1987) *A Child in Mind – Protection of Children in a Responsible Society: The report of the Commission of Inquiry into the death of Kimberley Carlisle.* London, London Borough of Greenwich

London Borough of Lambeth (1987) *Whose Child?: Report of the Inquiry into the death of Tyra Henry.* London, London Borough of Lambeth

London Child Protection Committee (2003) *London Child Protection Procedures.* London, Association of London Government

Lyon, C M (2000) *Loving Smack or Lawful Assault?: A contradiction in human rights and law*. London, Institute for Public Policy Research

Long, B and McLachlan, B (2002) *The Hunt for Britain's Paedophiles.* London, Hodder and Stoughton

Manthorpe, J (1999) *Institutional Abuse*. London, Routledge

Marchant, R (1993) *Bridging the Gap: Child protection work and children with multiple disabilities*. London, NSPCC

Mason-John, V.(2005) *Borrowed Body*. London,John Serpentstail Books

McGee, H (2002) *The Savi Report*. Dublin, The Liffey Press

Milner, P and Carolin, B (eds) (1999) *Time to Listen to Children: Personal and professional communication*. London, Routledge

Mullender, A (2002) *Children's Perspectives on Domestic Violence*. London, Sage

Mullender, A (2003) *Stop Hitting Mum: Children talk about domestic violence*. Surrey, Young Voice

Munro, E (1995) 'Common Errors of Reasoning in Child Protection Work', in *Child Abuse and Neglect*, Vol.23, No.8

Munro, E (1996) 'Avoidable and Unavoidable Mistakes in Child Protection Work', in *British Journal of Social Work*, XXVI, pp795-810

Munro E (2003) 'This would not have saved Victoria', in *Society Guardian*, 10 September 2003

Munro, E (2002) *Effective Child Protection*. London, Sage

Munro, E and Calder, M (2005) 'Where has child protection gone?' in *The Political Quarterly*, Vol.76, No.3, pp 439-445

Munro E (2006) *Child Protection*. London, Sage

Nazer, M (2004) *Slave: The true story of a girl's lost childhood and her fight for survival*. London, Virago

NSPCC (2001) *Fragile: Handle with Care*. London, NSPCC

NSPCC (2001) *Out of Sight: Report on child deaths from abuse 1973-2000*. London, NSPCC

O'Neale, V (2000) *Excellence Not Excuses: Inspection of services for ethnic minority children and families*. London, SSI DH Publications

Oliver, T and Smith, R (1993) *Lambs to the Slaughter: Operation Orchid investigation*. Herfordshire, TimeWarner Books

Parton, N (2005) *Safeguarding Childhood*. Hampshire, Palgrave

Peake, A and Fletcher, M (1997) *Strong Mothers: A resource for mothers of children who have been sexually assaulted*. Dorset, Russell House Publishing

Pearce, J et al (2002) *It's Someone Taking a Part of You: A study of young women and sexual exploitation*. London, NCB

Platt, D and Shemmings, D (1997) *Making Enquiries into Alleged Child Abuse and Neglect*. Brighton, Pavilion Publishing

Radford, L, Sayers, S and AMICA, (1999) *Unreasonable fears?* Bristol, Women's Aid Federation of England

Reder, P, Duncan, S and Gray, M (1993) *Beyond Blame – Child Abuse Tragedies Revisited: A summary of 35 Inquiries since 1973*. London, Routledge

Reder, P and Duncan, S (1999) *Lost Innocents: A follow-up study of fatal child abuse*. London, Routledge

Rees, G (2001) *Working with Runaways: Learning from practice*. London, The Children's Society

Report of the Inquiry into the Removal of Children from Orkney (1991). London, HMSO

Report of the Inquiry into Child Abuse in Cleveland (1988). London, HMSO

Richards, A and Ince, L (2002) *Quality Services for Looked After Children in Black and Ethnic Minority Children and their Families*. Family Rights Group [also available at www.adsss.org.uk/publications/other/ocomsum.shtml]

Saradjuan, J (1997) *Women Who Sexually Abuse Children*. Sussex, Wiley

Sereny, G (1998) *Cries Unheard: The story of Mary Bell*. London, Eyre Methuen

Sexual Offences Act (2003). London, TSO [also available at www. homeoffice.gov.uk/justice/sentencing/sexualoffencesbill]

Somerset, C (2001) *What the Professionals Know. The trafficking of children into and through the UK for sexual purposes*. London, ECPAT UK

Smith, K (2002) *Child Protection Investigator's Companion*. Bristol, The New Police Bookshop

Smith, G (1995) *The Protector's Handbook*. London, Women's Press:

Social Exclusion Unit (2002) *Report: Young Runaways*. London, ODPM [also available at www.socialexclusion.gov.uk/page.asp?id=52]

Taylor-Browne, J and Broadfoot, F (2002) *Voicing Our Views*. London, ECPAT UK

Victoria Climbié Inquiry Report (2003). London, TSO [the transcript of the Inquiry and witness statements are available at www.victoria-climbie-inquiry.org.uk]

Walker, A (1992) *Possessing the Secret of Joy*. London, Vintage

Warner, N (1992) *Choosing with Care: Report of the Committee of Inquiry into the selection, development and management of staff in children's homes*. London, HMSO

Welsh Office (2000) *Lost In Care: Report of the Tribunal of Inquiry into the abuse of children in care in the former county council areas of Gwynedd and Clwyd since 1974*. London, TSO

Westcott, H (1993) *Abuse of Children and Adults with Disabilities*. London, NSPCC

Wolmar, C (2000) *Forgotten Children: The secret abuse scandal in children's homes*. London, Vision

UNICEF (2003) *End Child Exploitation: Stop the Traffic!* London: UNICEF UK

UNICEF (2003) *End Child Exploitation: Facts and Figures*, London: UNICEF UK

Books for direct work with children

Bruzzone, C (1996) *All About Me*. Surrey, Small Publishing

Bruzzone, C (1996) *My Friends*. Surrey, Small Publishing

Bruzzone, C (1996) *The Family Tree*. Surrey, Small Publishing

Child Witness Pack (1998) London, NSPCC

Davies, D and Megale, M (1984) *Something Is Wrong at My House: A book about violence in the home*. Seattle, USA Parenting Press

Fiddy, A, Hamilton, C and Paton, L (2004) *At What Age Can I ?A guide to age-based legislation*. Essex, Children's Legal Centre

Freeman, L and Deach, C (1990) *It's MY Body: A book to teach young children how to resist uncomfortable touch*. New York, Fawcett Columbine

Green, J (2002) *What do we think about Racism?* London, Hodder Wayland

Ironside,V (2001) *The Huge Bag of Worries*. London, Hodder Wayland

Moore Campbell, B (2003) *Sometimes My Mummy Gets Angry*. New York, GP Putmans Sons

National Deaf Children's Society, *You Choose*. London, NDCS

National Deaf Children's Society, *Secrets*. London, NDCS

Rouf, K (1989) *Mousie*. London, The Children's Society

Rouf, K (1989) *Secrets*. London, The Children's Society

Peake, A and Rouf, K (1989) *My Body My Book*. London, The Children's Society

Pickering, F (2000) *Hitting and Hurting*. London, The Children's Society

Stones, R and Ludlow, P (2002) *No More Bullying*. London, Dinosaur

Striker, S and Kimmel, E (2004) *The Anti-Colouring Book*. New York, Scholastic

Taylor, C and Thompson Dicks, J (1992) *The House That Crack Built*. California, Chronicle Books

NSPCC (1997) *Turning Points: A resource pack for communicating with children*. London, NSPCC

UNICEF (2002) 'For Every Child: A children's version of the UN Convention' at www.unicef.org.uk

Vigna, J (1993) *I Wish Daddy Didn't Drink So Much*. Illinois, Albert Whitman Prairie

Videos

Home Truths (1999). See www.leedsanimation.org.uk

In Safe Hands (2001): Resource Pack to support work with refugee children. London, Save the Children

More Precious than Gold (2003). UNICEF, available at www.endchildexploitation.org.uk/robbiewilliams

No Son of Mine (2001): Video and training book about young men exploited through prostitution. Essex, Barnardo's

Sounding the Alarm (1998). Essex, Barnardo's

Towards Safer Care (2000). London, Department of Health

Two Way Street (2001): Training video and handbook about communicating with disabled children and young people. London, NSPCC

Whose Daughter Next?: Children abused through prostitution (1998). Essex. Barnardo's

Agencies and organisations involved in safeguarding children

A National Voice
Central Hall, Oldham St, Manchester M1 1JQ
0161 237 5577, 0207 833 9863 (London office)
www.anationalvoice.org
Gives a voice to children and young people who are or have been looked after

Ann Craft Trust
ACT Centre for Social Work, University of Nottingham, University Park, Nottingham NG7 2RD
0115 951 5400
www.anncrafttrust.org
National association for the protection from abuse of children and adults with learning disabilities

ACAL: Association of Child Abuse Lawyers
Suite 5, Claremont House, 22-4 Claremont Road, Surbiton KT6 4QU
0208 390 4701
www.childabuselawyers.com
Useful website for news reports and current legislation

ARCH : Action on Rights for Children
c/o 62 Wallwood Road, London E11 1AZ
0208 558 9317 (advice line)
www.arch-ed.org
Information and advice

Asylum Aid
28 Commercial Street, London E1 6LS
0207 247 8741 (advice line)
www.asylumaid.org.uk

Barnardo's
Tanner's Lane, Barkingside, Ilford, Essex 1G6 1QG
0208 550 8822
www.barnardo's.org.uk

Barnardo's Young Men's Project
3 Morocco Street, London SE1 3HB
020 7378 8797
Working against child sexual exploitation

Barnardo's Young Women's Project
PO Box 34727, London N7 8YQ
020 7700 2253, 0800 316 1770 (freephone)
Working against child sexual exploitation

BASPCAN: British Association for the Study and Prevention of Child Abuse and Neglect
10 Priory St, York YO1 6ET
01904 613605
www.baspcan.org.uk
Multi-disciplinary organisation for professionals working in child protection

BAAF: British Association for Adoption and Fostering
Saffron House, 6-10 Kirby Street, London EC1N 8TS
0207 421 2600
www.baaf.org.uk

Care Leavers Association
St Thomas Centre , Ardwick Green North , Manchester M12 6FZ
0161 275 9500
www.careleavers.com

Child and Woman Abuse Studies Unit (CWASU)
London Metropolitan University, Ladbroke House, 62-66 Highbury Grove, London N5 2AD
www.cwasu.org.uk

ChildLine
0800 1111
0800 400 222 text phone
www.childline.org.uk
Confidential helpline for children

Children's Legal Centre
University of Essex, Wivenhoe Park, Colchester C04 3SQ
01206 872 466
www.childrenslegalcentre.com
Free legal advice for young people.

Children are Unbeatable Alliance
94 White Lion Street, London N1 9PF
0207 713 0569
www.childrenareunbeatable.org.uk

Children's Rights Alliance for England
94 White Lion Street, London N1 9PF
0207 278 8222
www.crae.org.uk

The Children's Society
Edward Rudolf House, Margery Street, London WC1X OJL
0845 300 1128
www.childrenssociety.org.uk
Publications, resources and advice and young carers initiative

Christian Survivors of Sexual Abuse
BM CSSA London WCIN 3XX

CISters (Child incest survivors)
02380 338080
Support network for adult women who were sexually abused as children

Commission for Social Care Inspection CSCI
33 Greycoat Street,London SW1P 2QF
0845 015 0120, Textphone: 0845 015 2255
www.csci.org.uk
www.rights4me.org.uk (website for children and young people)

Council for Disabled Children
8 Wakeley Street, London EC1V 7QE
0207 843 6000
www.ncb.org.uk/cdc/
Services and support for children and young people with disabilities and special educational needs

Criminal Injuries Compensation Authority (CICA)
Morley House, 26-30 Holborn Viaduct, London, EC1A 2JQ
020 7842 6800, 0800358 3601 (helpline)
www.cica.gov.uk

CROA: Children's Rights Officers and Advocates
Suite 5J, North Mill, Bridgefoot, Belper, Derbyshire DE56 1YD
01773 820100
www.croa.org.uk
Provides voice for children looked after. Independent advice and support including the Total Respect Pack.

Eating Disorders Association
1st Floor Wensum House, 103 Prince of Wales Rd, Norwich NR1 1DW
01603619090, 01603 621414 (helpline)
www.edauk.com

ECPAT Coalition of Child Prostitution and Tourism
Grosvenor Gardens House, 35-7 Grosvenor Gardens, London
SW1W 0BS
0207 233 9887
www.ecpat.org.uk
Campaign against sex tourism and child trafficking

Family Rights Group
The Print House,18 Ashwin St, London E8 3DL
0207 923 2628
www.frg.org.uk
Provides legal and professional advice for families

Forced Marriages Abroad
The Community Liaison Unit G55, Foreign and Commonwealth Office,
Old Admiralty Building, London SW1A 2PA
020 7008 0151
www.fco.gov.uk
Advice and information

Further resources

Forward
765-7 Harrow Road, London NW10 5NY
0208 960 4000
www.forwarduk.co.uk
Campaign against and advice about female genital mutilation

Freedom to Care
PO Box 125B, West Molesey, Surrey KT8 1YE
0208 224 1022
www.freedomtocare.org

Grandparents Association
Moot House,The Stow,Harlow,Essex CM20 3AG
01279 428040, 01279 444964 (advice line)
www.grandparents-association.org.uk
Support for grandparents caring for grandchildren who have lost or are losing contact with parents

Homestart
www.home-start.org.uk
Free confidential advice to support families

Howard League
1 Ardleigh Road, London N1 4HS
0207 249 7373
www.howardleague.org.uk
Campaigns for and represents interests of young prisoners

Kidscape
2 Grosvenor Gardens London SW1W 0DH
0207 730 3300, 08451 205 204 (helpline)
www.kidscape.org.uk
Information on bullying and keeping children safe. Helpline for parents

Lucy Faithfull Foundation
Bordesley Hall, The Holloway, Alvechurch, Birmingham B48 7QA
01527 591922
Assessment, intervention and relapse prevention programmes for adult male sex abusers

Medical Foundation for the Victims of Torture
111 Isledon Road, Islington, London N7 7JW
0207 697 7777
www.torturecare.org.uk

Muslim Women's Helpline
020 8 904 8193, 0208 908 6715 (helpline)
www.mwhl.org
Counselling for muslim women over 16 yrs

NAPAC: National Association of People Abused in Childhood
9 Marshalsea Road, London SE1
0800 085 3330
www.napac.org.uk

National Deaf Children's Society
15 Dufferin Street, London EC1Y 8UR
0207 490 8656 (minicom), 0808 800 8880 (helpline)
www.ncds.org.uk

National Missing Persons Bureau
284 Upper Richmond Rd, London SW14 7JE
0208 392 4518, 0800 700 700 (message home helpline)
www.missingpersons.org

National Youth Advocacy Service
99-105 Argyle Street, Birkenhead, Wirral, CH41 6AD
0151 649 8700, 0800 616101 (young people's helpline)
www.nyas.net
Offers advocates for young people

NSPCC: National Society for the Prevention of Cruelty to Children
National Centre, 42 Curtain Road, London EC2A 3NH
0207 825 2500, 0800 800 500 (helpline)
www.nspcc.org.uk

Parentline Plus
0207 284 5500
www.parentlineplus.org.uk
Support for parents and carers

The Poppy Project
2nd Floor, Lincoln House, 1-3 Brixton Road, London SW9 6DE
0207 840 7129
www.poppy.ik.com
Develops and provides accommodation and support services to women who have been trafficked for sexual exploitation purposes and want to escape

Public Concern at Work
Suite 306, 16 Baldwin's Gardens, London EC1N 7RJ
0207 404 6609
www.pcaw.co.uk
Support for staff raising concerns – whistleblowing

The Refuge (St Christopher's Fellowship and NSPCC)
PO Box 3652, London N7 9HY
020 7700 7541, 0800 389 2168 (freephone)
Confidential short stay refuge for young people aged 11-16

Refugee Council
3-9 Bondway, London SW8 1SJ
0207 346 1134 (Children's Panel advice line), 0207 3346 6777 (The One Stop service)
www.refugeecouncil.org.uk
Assists newly arrived refugees

Refugee Legal Centre
153-7 Commercial Road, London E1 2DA
0207 780 3200
www.refugee-legal-centre.org.uk
Legal representation for children

Respond
3rd Floor, 24-32 Stephenson Way, London NW1 2HD
0207 383 0700, 0808 808 0700 (helpline)
www.respond.org.uk
Challenges vulnerability and sexual abuse in the lives of people with learning disabilities

SACCS: Sexual Abuse Care & Consultancy Service
Mytton Mill, Montford Bridge, Shrewsbury, Shropshire, SY4 1HA
01743 850015
www.saccs.co.uk
Professional advice and support

Save the Children: Centre for Young Children's Rights
356 Holloway Road, London N7 6PA
0207 700 8127
www.scfuk.org.uk
Information on children's rights and specialist resources for work with refugee children

Sexwise
0800 28 29 30 (helpline)
www.ruthinking.co.uk
Free, confidential advice on sex, relationships and contraception for anyone aged under 18

Stop It Now
PO Box 9841, Birmingham B48 7WB
01527 598184, 0808 1000900 (helpline)
www.stopitnow.org
Child abuse prevention group, with a helpline for adults concerned about their own behaviour towards children

Triangle
Unit E1, The Knoll Business Centre, Old Shoreham Road, Hove, East Sussex BN9 7GS
01273 413141
www.triangle-services.co.uk
Services for children with disabilities, including provision of the 'How It Is' image vocabulary as a communication tool for working with children with communication difficulties and child abuse

Who Cares? Trust
Kemp House, 152-160 City Road, London EC1V 2NP
0207 251 3117
www.thewhocarestrust.org.uk

Further resources

Witness
0845 4500 300
www.witnessagainstabuse.org.uk
Support and advocacy for survivors of abuse by professionals

Women's Aid Foundation
PO Box 391, Bristol, BS99 7WS
0117 963 4411, 0808 2000 247 (helpline)
www.womensaid.org.uk
www.thehideout.org.uk (resource for women and children)

www.no2abuse.com
Survivors' website

www.thinkuknow.co.uk
Website with information for adults and children about staying safe online

Voice UK
Wyvern House, Railway Terrace, Derby DE1 2RU
01332 295775
www.voiceuk.org.uk
Support group for children and adults with disabilities who have experienced crimes or abuse

Young Abusers Project, NSPCC
The Peckwater Resource Centre, 6 Peckwater Street, London, NW5 2TX
020 7 530 6467
Agency to assess/treat young people who sexually abuse

YoungMinds
48-50 St John Street, London EC1M 4DG
0207 336 8445, 0800 018 2138 (free helpline)
www.youngminds.org.uk
Provide a free confidential helpline for anyone with concerns about a young person and mental health issues

Printed in the United Kingdom
by Lightning Source UK Ltd.
123629UK00001B/31-42/A